JEWISH WARRIORS

A Compact Introduction to Real-Life
Action Heroes from the Tribe

Ross Berg

Photography by E.A. Schwartz
Illustrations by Ken Mills

Jewish Warriors: A Compact Introduction to Real-Life Action Heroes from the Tribe
Copyright © 2020 Ross Berg
All rights reserved.

Cover Design by M. Berg

ISBN: 9798576555581

EMERGING INK SOLUTIONS
Kara Scrivener, Editor
www.emergingink.com

To my beautiful wife and wonderful children

"Jewish heroes must be brought to the attention of Jewish
youngsters."

Rabbi Meir Kahane
Never Again! A Program for Survival

ACKNOWLEDGEMENTS

A most gracious thank you to Fern Sidman who acted as my inspiration and muse for the duration of this project. Thank you, Fern, for being such an invaluable resource. You have cheered me on every step of the way, provided me priceless firsthand accounts and memories, and supplied one-of-a-kind photographs. Your generosity of spirit is inspiring and you have, indeed, become the inspiration for the book itself. I can never thank you enough; I can only hope to honor your legacy – and the special league of Warriors to which you belong – through my words.

Additional heartfelt gratitude goes to E.A. Schwartz for generously allowing me to use the amazing photos of Rabbi Meir Kahane and The Jewish Defense League seen within the pages of this book. Your belief in this project since day one has been empowering. Thank you for your special documentation of a profound chapter in our Jewish history. God bless you, my friend.

All E.A. Schwartz photos of The JDL in this book are from 1975.

I thank the following people for their love, support, and inspiration throughout the life of this project; please forgive me if I have forgotten anyone:

Avi Abelow, Buzz Alpert, Ze'ev Bar-El, Aline Bohm Greif, the Bravos, Cantor Ken, Levi Chazen, Melissa Cohen, Doug-Matt-Brian, the Eisenbergs, Estelle and Jimmy, Ari Fuld, the Gils,

Nir Goldenberger, Aharon Hadida, Herut Zionists, Dov
Hikind, Lauren Isaacs, Libby Kahane, Moshe Katz, Eva
Kor, Sara Lee, the Lehmanns, Chaia Leib, Rivkah Levin,
Tom Messchendorp, Ken Mills, Mom and Dad, Doris
Wise Montrose, the Morenos, Aaron N.: My Hebro,
Adam Nierenberg, Omi and Opi, Paula K. Pacente,
Desiree Phillips, Ros Radley, Kandy Rock, Erin Mabel
Rodriguez, Shelley Rubin, Efraim Shapiro, Dina Shira,
Valerie Sobel, the Solomons, the Stevens, Meir Halevi
Weinstein, Evan Winer, Yeshiva of the Jewish Idea.

TABLE OF CONTENTS

INTRODUCTION

"If you hold a permanent view of yourself as a victim, you become your own oppressor."

Candace Owens, Commentator/Activist

I was eight years old in 1977 and had only recently learned about something called the Holocaust from a film shown to us at Temple, which depicted naked, battered, and lifeless bodies being maneuvered around by farming equipment. I hadn't expected to see the film and, traumatized, upon returning home told my parents what I had witnessed. From there, my parents had little choice but to fill in the blanks and further explain to me about Hitler, the concentration camps, and the Jew-hating Nazis. In my need to find out more, I began secretly thumbing through the books in my parents' collection – and viewing photographs of severed heads and charred bodies from the camps. I saw photos of Nazis laughing as they cut off the beards of orthodox rabbis while publicly humiliating them in the streets. I studied images of German soldiers smiling and posing proudly next to dead Jewish bodies hanging by their necks from trees like hunters with their trophies.

The whole thing shook me to my core.

The next year, a movie called *The Holocaust*, starring Meryl Streep and James Woods, was aired on NBC television. It was decided that I was too young to watch, but my parents allowed my older cousin to view the program. It affected him profoundly, prompting him to move back into the bedroom we had shared a year earlier so he wouldn't be alone at night.

The next day I went to school and my best friend said, "Did you see the TV last night? They put all these Jews on a train and sent them off to die." Completing his observation, he began laughing. I didn't know how to react, realizing then that this thing that touched me and my family members so deeply was not necessarily experienced in the same painful way by people who weren't Jewish.

I began to notice little things, like the way my parents hung our Mezuzah on the inside of the front door rather than displaying it publicly on the outside of the home as is the custom. Fear seemed to be the predominant emotion around all of this – fear and perhaps some sense of shame, knowing now that I was a member of a victimized group.

Around this same time, I remember my parents speaking of something called **The Jewish Defense League** at dinner one night. I was enthralled as they regaled my cousin and me with tales of tough, young Members of the Tribe escorting elderly Jews – many of whom were Holocaust survivors – to and from Temple so they wouldn't be mugged or terrorized. I remember my cousin exclaiming, "I'm going to join The Jewish Defense League when I grow up!" and seeing an immediate change in him. I idolized my cousin and so decided that I too would one day join this courageous group of Jewish Warriors alongside him.

My mother often retold the story of her brother, an enlisted Navy seaman, punching a fellow soldier in the face and breaking the man's jaw in the process for telling one too many Jew jokes. In light of these stories, previous notions I had formed of an unalterable fate defined by weakness and victimization began to shift. With excitement and admiration, I watched as my cousin actively sought out swastikas scrawled onto walls and schoolyard desks and – with a few strokes of his pen – effectively transformed these putrid symbols of hate into innocuous, box-shaped window patterns by drawing a border atop the offending designs. My cousin took action and turned his fear into empowerment. His display of action – of blotting out symbols that were designed to make our community feel small, victimized, degraded, and shamed – left an indelible mark on me. I felt pride and so decided I wanted only to feel pride in being a Jew from then on.

I felt pride, yes; still, the status of being Jewish seemed ever-entwined with the burden of gauging when and how to handle the anti-Semitism around me. How far was I expected to go in this fight? Was every slight worth war, especially when I was greatly outnumbered? How much did I want to define myself as an outsider during those teenage years where peer acceptance was of such supreme importance?

There were times when I was strong and felt vindicated in my swift action: the first day of middle school came complete with a schoolyard bully taunting me with the words "Jew Boy" and me, in turn, grabbing him by the throat until he apologized. I was never bothered again by him or anyone else for the next three years of my middle school experience and the result was a clear example of "peace through strength." Once potential bullies knew I would fight back if provoked, they looked elsewhere for easier prey. But, as is the case with most everyone, there were also days when I felt weak and utterly outnumbered.

In my senior year of high school, a Holocaust survivor visited and spoke with our predominantly non-

Jewish student body about her harrowing experiences. She revealed to us that after many hours in a cattle car, she drank her own urine in a moment of desperate and maddening thirst. The students instantly responded with exclamations of "Yuck!" and "Eww!" and before long, the room erupted into laughter. It was one of the worst moments of my life – I can't imagine how the speaker felt.

I don't recall what happened next. I don't remember if the teachers called the group to order or if they went on to scold the crowd. I don't remember what the reaction of the poor woman was, if she cried, left the room, or stayed strong in the face of such cruel and outrageous insensitivity. All I know is I despised every one of those students for doing what they did to her and I hated myself even more for not standing up to them. I was filled with rage and shame and I disconnected psychologically and the rest of that memory is blank. It was another jarring realization that this thing that touched me and my People so deeply was not necessarily experienced in the same painful way by those who were not Jewish.

Growing up, I attended Hebrew school, went to Jewish summer camp, and was fortunate enough to visit the Anne Frank House on a family trip to Amsterdam – my pride in being a Jew and my preoccupation with the Holocaust never fading. As a youth, I felt extreme pride in discovering that my favorite rock star, Gene Simmons, was a fellow Jew. It was empowering to see such a fierce persona linked to the "People of the Book" and I took great joy in seeing Gene physically battle enemies in the KISS fantasy film

released in 1978. My fascination took on greater
dimensions upon learning that Gene's mother had
survived Nazi concentration camps.

Ultimately, my keen interest led me to author a
book about the death camps and traits of children of
Holocaust survivors, with Gene's story and celebrity
serving as enticement for people who might not otherwise
care to read about such a topic. The responses I received
from Jews and non-Jews alike were inspiring with many
non-Jews indeed admitting that the Holocaust was a
subject they either hadn't known or particularly cared
about before reading my book. Such feedback made the
six years of sleepless nights it took to complete the work
worth it.

Writing the book brought me closer to my religion
and to the Holocaust than I had ever previously ventured.
The result was ultimately a career change – a calling to
serve the Jewish community that simply could not be
ignored. After 15 years, I left my job as a college counselor
to dive heart and soul into work as a Temple
Administrator for a beautiful and historic Shul.

One of the most satisfying aspects of my job was
the ability to have an impact on the safety of the Temple
and its congregants. I experienced profound satisfaction in
being in close contact with the local police department and
former members of the **Israeli Defense Forces** to better
secure the safety of our Temple members. The deep
interest I have in being a protector of my People seems, in
my mind, to have a direct connection to those riveting
tales of The Jewish Defense League my parents spun
around the dinner table those many years ago when I was
a kid.

But what was The Jewish Defense League, really?
Who started it and who were the people who joined? I
really hadn't a clue. I had my parents' stories and a few

memories from my childhood. As a teenager, around the time of my Bar Mitzvah, the Reform Temple I attended invited a controversial figure to speak to the community. I cannot recall who the speaker was, but he advocated for Israel to relinquish sections of its God-given Land in the Middle East conflict; The Jewish Defense League (JDL) turned out in force.

For weeks after, the congregation was abuzz about the appearance of its leader, **Irv Rubin**. Not everyone agreed with Irv's views, but all had been touched by the absolute force of his convictions and his electrifying presence during the protest. I remember that as an early "brush with greatness" with regards to The JDL, Irv Rubin had actually stalked the outer steps of my childhood Temple fighting for the rights of Israel!

I also recall my uncle telling me he saw JDL Founder **Rabbi Meir Kahane** (pronounced 'Kuh – HAWN – Uh') speak once at the University of California, Los Angeles. Standing alone at a lectern on a large stage, the aging Rabbi had kept the hall captivated with his passionate words; my uncle recalled it as being the most mesmerizing experience of his life, leaving him literally unable to turn away even as he didn't agree with everything he heard. I only wish I could have been there to witness it.

And so, at middle age I found myself still completely captivated and preoccupied with the Holocaust, Jewish power and pride, the safety and security of my People, and something called The Jewish Defense League. In short, I believed I had the topic for my next book. My first task was to thoroughly explore the writings of JDL Founder

Rabbi Meir Kahane. Some people had cautioned me against studying "The Fighting Rabbi," stating that he had been a vigilante fanatic, but as I began reading his story, I became enamored with his conviction and obvious love for the Jewish People.

The Rabbi was always careful in delineating between vigilantism and defense and refuted his opponents' claims that violence was 'un-Jewish.' Before taking action in any area of his life, he asked the simple question: "Is it good for the Jews?"

Kahane fought for the survival and freedoms of Soviet Jewry with a focus and intensity that was sorely lacking in the reactions of American-Jewish leaders during the Holocaust. The result of his tireless efforts was the successful emigration of tens of thousands of oppressed Jews from the Soviet Union. With wit, with anger, and with great humanity, Rabbi Kahane challenged us to examine the perils of assimilation, the dangers of remaining silent in the face of evil, and how the new strong Jew of The JDL was really the old heroic Jew of the Torah reborn.

Kahane's passages about Jewish merchants being robbed and terrorized by thugs in what once had been Jewish neighborhoods struck a personal chord as I recalled stories of my grandfather on my father's side, who owned a liquor store in the 1960s, struggling daily to keep from being burglarized and worse. His store was ultimately looted and burned to the ground in a neighborhood riot.

Around the same time, my maternal grandmother was violently mugged in her once-Jewish neighborhood and, consequently, left her home less and less frequently. As such episodes of violence toward innocent Jewish merchants and the elderly – many of them Holocaust survivors – increased in the late 1960s and early 1970s, Rabbi Kahane and his Jewish Defense League rose up to protect their People, effectively becoming guardian angels of many a troubled neighborhood.

Kahane's philosophy was simple: a Jew in trouble should never go un-aided by a fellow Jew. If a Jew had the financial means to flee a dangerous and poverty-stricken neighborhood, he still carried the burden and responsibility of helping the Jew who was left behind.

I found Meir Kahane's philosophies to be thought-provoking and inspiring. He challenged the Jewish People to make sacrifices to help one another. He demanded that the comfortable Jew face uncomfortable questions and to help the fellow Jew who had yet to find comfort.

I purchased Kahane-penned books and borrowed them from the library and discovered I couldn't wait to devour the wisdom of their pages each night as I returned home from work. I found the Rabbi's words speaking both *to* me and *for* me, the power of his honesty resonating deep down in my Jewish gut.

If the Rabbi's book *Never Again!* had been standard, required reading for all of us in Hebrew School when we were 11 or 12 years old, how different might our relationships with our religion and our People have been as a result? How many of us might have walked a little taller and prouder? How many of us might have had a truer understanding of what our Bar/Bat Mitzvahs really meant? How many of us would have felt more confident in explaining to others what our relationship to Israel was and why that connection is so vital? How many of us might have proudly declared who we really were instead of keeping it a secret to fit in with society? How many of us would have joined a pro-Israel organization in high school or college and taken advantage of the Birthright Program? How many of us might have joined or financially supported JDL? How many of us would have taken to the streets when Irv Rubin was falsely imprisoned to demand his release?

How many of us might have learned to ask the most important of questions:

"Is it good for the Jews?"

This is the yardstick for acting or not acting in this life, regardless of whether or not the decision is a turn-off to polite society. Rabbi Kahane sought to shake the Jewish community out of its historically frightened and apathetic stance of not wanting to "make waves." To the many in polite society who felt it was not dignified for the Jew to sink to the level of violence – even in the case of self-defense – the Rabbi asserted that there was nothing dignified in letting your enemies enslave you… and that there was nothing morally elevated in allowing your enemies to kill you.

What a sad thing that to this day, the teachings of Rabbi Kahane are considered extreme or fringe. What a tragic revelation to think that his teachings could very well energize a new generation of young Jews that will, sadly, never read his important words or ideas.

It's not too late. Maybe they still can learn.

Maybe they can learn not only about the Rabbi but discover his connection to the greatest Warriors of our past and realize that they themselves are every bit a part of the heroic legacy of the Jewish People – that they are, in fact, modern-day Maccabees, should they choose to be.

The past and the future await you in these pages.

It's not too late.

PREFACE

KEY PRINCIPLES OF THE JEWISH WARRIOR

"I am not a Jew with trembling knees."

Menachem Begin, Prime Minister of Israel

In 1968, elderly Jews in New York were routinely harassed and robbed while walking home from Synagogue; many of these victims had lived through the horrors of the Holocaust. In response, a courageous man named Rabbi Meir Kahane formed The Jewish Defense League, an organization made up of strong, young Jews who would provide physical protection for those vulnerable to assault.

Rabbi Kahane began mentoring these Jewish Warriors , instilling in them five key principles:

1. *Ahavat Yisrael* – "Love of Israel and the Jewish People:" Whenever and wherever a fellow Jew is hurt, we should do everything in our power to help him or her.
2. *Hadar* – "Dignity and Pride:" A proud Jew should possess self-esteem and show anti-Semites that they cannot attack a Jew without getting hurt.
3. *Barzel* – "Iron Strength:" A Jew should train and know how to fight for the sake of self-defense or in defense of fellow Jews.

4. *Mishmaat* – "Discipline and Unity:" Jews may not agree on everything but, in the end, we have to unite in order to survive.
5. *Bitachon* – "Faith in the Indestructibility of the Jewish People:" The absolute realization that it is God's miracles that have saved the Jewish People from annihilation.

Eager to reach young Jewish people everywhere, Rabbi Kahane visited universities and spoke to college students on campus grounds and dorm rooms. To his dismay, time and time again, the Rabbi found that these Jewish students had decorated their college room walls with posters of revolutionary rebels and civil rights heroes, none of whom were Jewish and some of whom actually held anti-Jewish viewpoints.

Rabbi Meir Kahane, Founder of The Jewish Defense League

It was apparent to the Rabbi that these young Jews were starved for heroes, strong revolutionary, outspoken, courageous figures in whom to feel pride and connection. As these students had no awareness of any such figures to admire within their own Tribe, they simply sought heroes elsewhere. This struck Kahane as tragic as Jewish history is overflowing with examples of brave Warriors – both men and women – who fought time and time again to rise up and defend their People against ruthless enemies. The adventures of these great action heroes are compelling, but the details of their incredible bravery have very often failed to reach younger generations who so desperately need to revel in the connection.

Rabbi Kahane never gave up trying to fill the next generation with pride; he knew the future of his People depended upon it. Sadly, the great Rabbi's work went unfinished as his life ended abruptly. But we can carry his Warrior spirit into the modern age by learning about him and other Jewish heroes who led courageous lives of example. We can follow in their footsteps by allowing their courageous examples to live inside of us, filling our hearts and souls with strength and pride each day.

Let us take a journey through history – from the time of the Bible to the present day – and celebrate the myriad of Warriors who comprise the Jewish People. In every example, the Almighty stood, and stands, firmly beside His Chosen People as they battle their enemies.

Our journey begins...

1

REAL-LIFE SUPERHEROES: WARRIORS OF

BIBLICAL TIMES

"Our great Jews — Moses, King David, Samson, the Maccabees — were Jews who fought back when they were being spiritually or physically threatened."

Irv Rubin, National Chairman of The Jewish Defense League

What a beautiful thing it is to see the next generation of Jewish boys and girls emerging to learn the traditions and values of our People.

What a powerful image it is to view the next generation of Jewish boys and girls emerging as the living embodiment of Adolph Hitler's failed plan to eliminate our People from the very face of the earth.

And yet, understandably and most assuredly, the next generation must have questions and concerns regarding their faith and identity.

Perhaps they enjoy some of the holidays, spending time with family, eating good food, and receiving presents.

Perhaps they have come to the realization that they belong to a religious minority group.

Perhaps they feel a spiritual connection to God.

Perhaps they find their Sunday school boring and would rather be playing video games or watching the latest Marvel action movie.

Would it surprise them to know that Jewish history is filled with many exciting battles and adventures similar to those very video games and comic book films?

Would it surprise them to know that, historically, the Jewish People are some of the bravest Warriors the world has ever known?

As Jews, we are related to a multitude of real-life superheroes that dates back to the time of the Holy Bible, men and women who put the fantastic but utterly imaginary exploits of comic book characters to shame with their actual heroics and daring.

Jewish Pioneers of the Comic Book Action Hero Genre

Interestingly, many great comic book superheroes were created by Jews. Jerome Siegel and Joseph Shuster, Jack Kirby, and Stan Lee all devoted their careers to teaching young people the virtues of being a hero. Of course, long before Siegel and Shuster drew a fictional Superman lifting a car with one hand, the very real **Samson** was tearing a vicious, charging lion apart limb from limb with his bare hands and striking 1,000 men into submission with a single blow with long, flowing hair, the source of his amazing strength.

Utilizing swords and spears, bows and arrows, clubs and axes, daggers and body armor, our Jewish ancestors were brave fighters who were prepared to protect important traditions and the God-given land of Israel.

God is a Zionist; He chose a Land and a People at an exact instant in time that made Judaism and Israel one and the same and thus inseparable from one another. **Abraham** was the very first Jew. A mighty Warrior, he was the first person to recognize the one true God. The Holy Bible is the oldest Title Deed in the world and states unequivocally the

Abraham: The first Jew and mighty warrior

Jewish right to the Land of Israel, providing clear boundaries and jurisdictions for the Land. When the Land the Almighty promised His People was threatened, Abraham assembled a makeshift army of just a few hundred men and led them into battle against the armies of four kings! This act of bravery kicked off a wave of other Biblical Jewish action heroes to follow.

Often, the Lord's supernatural plans guaranteed victory for the Warriors and the Children of Israel.

Joshua led the Israelites to blow their rams' horns and raise their mighty voices to bring down the imposing Walls of Jericho.

Deborah led the Israelites' charge down Mount Tabor toward the Canaanite Army as a great rain caused foes' chariots to struggle in the mud and overturn.

Gideon and a few hundred Israelites surrounded and surprised a giant army of Midianites in the dark of night with blaring trumpets, flaming torches, and victorious shouting, tricking the more numerous enemy forces to believe they were outnumbered and causing them to retreat.

Nehemiah taught his workers and followers to always hold a tool in one hand and a weapon in the other, as there is nothing an anti-Semite fears more than a Jew who fights back.

The pages of Jewish history are filled with a multitude of colorful, courageous, and tenacious characters; let us shed some light on key Bible heroes and the ways in which they shaped the course of Jewish history with their bravery and devotion to God.

2

MOSES

"Thou shalt not stand idly by your brother's blood."

Leviticus 19:16, The Holy Bible

In a time of great famine, an Israelite named Joseph used his dreams to save Egypt. Upon ascending the throne, however, the subsequent pharaoh expressed wariness for the children of Israel. Fearing the Israelites were becoming too numerous and strong, the pharaoh decreed that every Hebrew baby boy be thrown into the river.

Not far from the pharaoh's palace, a woman named Jochebed gave birth to a Hebrew baby in a little hut; she knew his life was in great danger. Making a basket of reeds, she and her daughter Miriam laid the baby gently into the basket-boat and prayed that God would protect him as the currents drew him from their outstretched hands.

It was at this time that the pharaoh's daughter was preparing to bathe near the river and spotted the reed basket among the rushes. She pulled the babe into her arms, declaring, "I will keep you and raise you as my own. I shall call you Moses."

Watching from the tall reeds, Miriam found the courage to come forward and bowed to the princess, saying, "Your baby looks hungry, O Princess. Shall I find a Hebrew woman to nurse the child for you?"

"Yes," the princess replied. "And when he is old enough, you are to bring Moses to me in the palace." Miriam excitedly returned to her mother Jochebed with baby Moses; not only had the child been saved, but he would be raised by his own mother.

In his years growing up in the palace of the pharaoh, Moses was treated as an Egyptian prince but secretly knew that he was really a Hebrew. Watching his brethren toil around him as beaten and degraded slaves filled Moses with great unhappiness and eventual rage. One day while watching the Hebrew slaves haul giant stones, Moses saw a worker fall under the weight of a rock. Too weak to rise, the slave cowered under the blows of a whip as an Egyptian guard screamed, "On your feet, you lazy slave!"

Moses ran to the Hebrew and demanded the guard leave the injured man alone, but the Egyptian continued to savagely beat the slave. Moses turned to see if anyone else would come to the aid of the suffering Hebrew, but no one moved. Determined not to stand idly by his brother's blood, Moses struck the Egyptian guard who fell to the ground dead.

Violence, while never good, is sometimes necessary. In striking down the brutal Egyptian, Moses upheld the principle that when one Jew is in pain, all Jews are in pain – and we are, therefore, obligated to do all that is necessary to aid and defend that fellow Jew.

Moses aiding and defending a fellow Jew

Afterward, God selected Moses as the Shepherd of the Children of Israel. Aided by the Lord, Moses boldly demanded that the pharaoh release the Israelites from bondage; they crossed the Red Sea to safety and, at Mount Sinai, received the Ten Commandments: the guiding principles of the Jewish faith.

3

KAHANE KORNER: AIDING AND DEFENDING

FELLOW JEWS

"Moses taught the Jew how to behave in times of suffering - - he didn't create a committee to study the root causes of Egyptian anti-Semitism. Moses, our teacher, used violence to aid a Jew."

Rabbi Meir Kahane, Founder of The Jewish Defense League

When Moses witnessed a fellow Jew being beaten, he took action against the injustice rather than passively observing. Rabbi Kahane pointed to Moses extensively in his writings and speeches as a great leader and teacher who modeled for the

Rabbi Meir Kahane and The Jewish Defense League take to the streets

Jewish People the use of *Barzel* (Iron Strength) to aid a fellow Jew in peril.

When a Jew fights back, he alters the Jewish image of the easy victim.

When a Jew fights back, she teaches the anti-Semite that Jewish blood is not cheap.

When a Jew fights back to protect life and property, that Jew informs the anti-Semite that he is in danger of losing his life and property.

When we refuse to allow the Jew-hater to shame and degrade us, we stand tall and are filled with pride, self-respect, and dignity known as *Hadar*.

4

DAVID

"We don't thrive on military acts. We do them because we have to, and thank God we are efficient."

Golda Meir, Prime Minister of Israel

As a young boy tending his father's sheep, David was approached by a lion that snatched a lamb from the flock. David quickly seized upon the lion and saved the lamb. As the lion turned to attack David, the boy aimed his slingshot at the beast and struck it directly between the eyes, killing it.

David was also known to play sweet music on his shepherd lap harp and dedicated his songs to the Lord and His goodness. One day, young David was asked to play his beautiful music before King Saul, who had fallen under a spell of sadness. The music that flowed from David's harp caused the king's eyes to brighten. Subsequently, the boy was invited to live with the king.

One morning, King Saul awoke to find the Philistines were once again gathering to make war against his People. The king's brave army of Israelites assembled to meet the challenge.

Separated by a narrow valley, the Israelites stood on one side of the hill while the Philistines faced them on the other. Just as young David

arrived to aid in the fight, a ten-foot-tall giant named
Goliath – outfitted in armor– strode from the Philistine
lines. Holding an enormous spear, the behemoth of a man
bellowed in a thunderous voice, "I declare this challenge
to the armies of Israel! Send one man to fight me! If this
man kills me, then the Philistines will be your servants! If I
kill this man, the Israelites will be our servants!" The
Israelite soldiers peered at one another, but no one moved
to accept the challenge.

Finally, young David stepped forward and shouted
to the giant, "You dare mock the army of the living God?
I will fight you myself!" The giant let out a thunderous
laugh as King Saul rushed to his beloved David.

"You cannot go up against this giant; you are just a
boy," the king implored. David spoke earnestly to the
king, explaining that just as the Lord had once protected
him from the vicious lion, God would also save him from
the vicious Philistine.

At that, King Saul stepped aside so the boy could
grab his slingshot. David ran down into the valley
separating the two armies. The giant, roaring with laughter
at the sight of David holding his tiny wooden weapon,
shouted, "Am I a dog that you come at me with sticks?
Come and I will give your flesh to the beasts of the fields!"

David, loading a stone into his weapon, replied,
"You come to me with a sword and a spear, but I come to
you in the name of the Lord God whom you have defied!"
With that, he slung the stone at Goliath's head, striking
him between the eyes. The giant crumpled to the ground
with enormous force. Standing over Goliath, David drew
the giant's sword from his belt and killed the man.

David never really knew Goliath's strength; he was
too focused on God's.

Witnessing the death of their champion, the Philistines fled in terror and the Israelites gave chase, pursuing them to the gates of their cities.

David goes into battle against Goliath

David was a great Warrior and became a captain of 10,000 men, winning many more victories against the Philistine armies. Eventually, David became King of Israel and made Jerusalem the capital of all the land. King David ruled for many years, writing beautiful songs in God's praise for the rest of his days.

5

KAHANE KORNER: JEWS AND WEAPONS

"Nothing says 'Never Again' like an armed Jew."

Jews Can Shoot (jewscanshoot.com)

David defeated a seemingly insurmountable enemy through the expert use of a projectile weapon, an ancient version of a firearm.
How would David have fared in his battle against Goliath had he been unarmed?
All of the world's tyrannical dictators – including Stalin, Mao, Castro, and Hitler – succeeded in oppressing people by ensuring that only the government had access to firearms. The Nazis knew it would be far easier to round up the Jews, force them into cattle cars, tear their children from their arms, and march them into gas chambers if those Jews were unarmed and thus unable to fight back.
If the **Warsaw Ghetto Uprising** proved anything, it was that if a few hundred Jewish fighters could hold off the armed forces of Nazi Germany for almost a month with only a handful of weapons, then certainly six million Jews armed with rifles could have prevented or greatly hampered the attempted extermination of their People.
As Adolph Hitler's genocidal plans for the Jewish People began to take shape, **Ze'ev Jabotinsky** raced throughout Europe, beseeching his fellow Jews to learn to operate firearms. As his spiritual successor, Rabbi Meir Kahane continued Jabotinsky's work, encouraging the

Jewish People to learn self-defense and coining the phrase "Every Jew, a .22."

Soon after The Jewish Defense League was established in the late-1960s, firearms and self-defense training camps were created and offered to thousands of Jews as part of JDL's platform of Jewish self-preservation. These programs continue all over the world to this day and instill our People with a knowledge, proficiency, and respect for firearms usage.

The mission of Rabbi Meir Kahane and The Jewish Defense League was, and is, centered on Jewish survival. When Rabbi Kahane famously announced, "Never Again!" he did not mean that a Holocaust would never again occur, but that *never again* would the Jewish People allow anyone to persecute and murder them unopposed. Never again would they be afraid, unprepared, or unarmed.

In the mid-1980s, as Rabbi Kahane was in the midst of a political career in Israel, Irv Rubin picked up the mantle of JDL leadership in America and continued to advocate for self-defense programs and firearms training courses for the Jewish People. His proclamation of "Jews: Stay Alive With a .45" built on Rabbi Kahane's earlier message of self-preservation. Its impact is still felt today through such organizations as **Jews Can Shoot**. A Jewish Second Amendment civil rights group, Jews Can Shoot serves to educate and spread the message that Jews support and practice the right to bear arms. With the slogan "There Are Six Million Reasons Why Jews Should Be Against Gun Control," this important organization reminds people of the community that genocide, tyranny, dictatorships, and the Holocaust all began with the disarmament of citizens.

Jews can shoot – whether that be one Jew learning the basics of rifle safety and proficiency in order to protect her family or her synagogue or the entirety of the Israeli Defense Forces keeping enemies and terrorists at bay each and every day, we will never be defenseless again.

There are some in this world who are uncomfortable with the idea of an armed Jewish populace or the notion that Israel has one of the strongest armies on the face of the Earth; to this, Rabbi Kahane famously remarked: "I prefer a powerful and proud Jewish State that is hated by the entire world than an Auschwitz that is loved by one and all."

Above & Adjacent: Members of The JDL practicing firearms techniques and safety

6

ESTHER

"Silence in the face of evil is, itself, evil."

Unknown, though generally credited to Dietrich Bonhoeffer

Esther and her cousin Mordecai lived in Shushan, the capital of Persia. One day, King Ahasuerus sent word through the lands of the kingdom that he was searching for a queen. Esther's beauty was known far and wide and the king's messengers soon came to find her to present her to the king. Before King Ahasuerus placed the crown upon her head, her cousin advised Esther to keep her Jewish background a secret as many in the court were hostile to the Hebrews. To do this, Esther hid her relationship with Mordecai, a well-known Jewish man.

Soon after Esther became queen, the king promoted an arrogant and disdainful man named Haman to the highest office in the land. Each day as he passed through the king's gate, Haman delighted to see the people bow to the ground before him. But one man refused to bow before Haman; that man was Mordecai.

"As a Jew, I only bow to the ground before God," Mordecai explained to the enraged Haman. In his fury, Haman decided he would not only punish Mordecai, but that he would destroy all the Jews in the Persian Empire.

Haman presented his idea to the king and sweetened the proposition by vowing to deposit 10,000 talents of silver into the king's treasury. "Fine," King Ahasuerus answered casually with the wave of his hand. "Do with the Jews whatever you think best."

Haman's death decree to the Jewish People spread throughout the land. Mordecai rushed to Queen Esther and urged her to go to the king and plead for her People's survival. But in Persia, it was the law that no one, not even the queen herself, could go before the king unless specifically requested to do so.

"If I appear uninvited before the king, his guards will put me to death," Queen Esther told Mordecai.

"Perhaps God made you queen for such a time as this," her cousin pleaded. "Perhaps you were selected so that your People might not perish."

Upon hearing those words, Queen Esther summoned the strength and bravery of her Warrior ancestors and went to appear uninvited before the king. Throwing the doors to the court wide open, Esther entered boldly as the king and his courtiers turned in shock and surprise. An army of guards

Queen Esther risks her life to save her People

surrounded Esther and swords bore down on her throat.

The king strode toward Esther and waved off his armed men. "What is your wish, my queen?"

As the guards returned their swords to their sheathes, Esther replied: "If it pleases the king, I have prepared a banquet, a banquet for the king and for Haman."

The king accepted the invitation and Haman hurried to the evening feast. At the event, Esther rose from the table and bravely spoke: "Oh my king, if I have found favor in your eyes, let my life be spared and the life of my People. For we have been sold, I and my People, to be destroyed, to be slain, to perish."

Looking at Esther in amazement, the king asked, "Who? Who is the man who would dare do this?"

Pointing to Haman, Esther cried, "This enemy! The wicked Haman!" The King commanded that Haman be hung from the very gallows that had been prepared for Mordecai. And the Jews were saved. As the good news was spread to every corner of the kingdom, the Jews of Persia rejoiced and thanked the Lord.

Members of The JDL celebrate Queen Esther's heroism during Purim

Members of The JDL celebrate Queen Esther's heroism during Purim

7

KAHANE KORNER: JEWISH IDENTITY AND PRIDE

"Even JDLers who ordinarily didn't wear a yarmulke made sure to put one on...to prove that it was no longer an invitation to an easy hit but a symbol of the tough and fearless Jew."

Yossi Klein Halevi, American-born Israeli Author and Journalist

Although she initially kept her Jewish identity a secret, Queen Esther finally identified herself as a Jew in order to save her People – and did so with courage and pride. Jewish identity is an important issue and a common symbol of that identity in modern times is a yarmulke.

The earliest Jewish reference to the covering of the head with a yarmulke, or skullcap, is found in Exodus 28:4 and is viewed as an expression of one's reverence for God and as a reminder of the Lord's ever-hovering presence.

Although the wearing of the yarmulke is not commanded by religious law, it has become a defining custom, largely to remind the Jew that his special faith separates him from secular society. At times, that defining visual symbol of otherness has led the Jew wearing the yarmulke to be a target of anti-Semitic harassment; Rabbi Kahane and The Jewish Defense League aimed to reverse that unfortunate fact.

The yarmulke is often associated with one who is devout and religiously studious. Jews are known as the "People of the Book." Although we have a Warrior heritage, we also have a scholarly one as we are commanded to read from and study Torah. The images of the physical Jewish Warrior and of the studious Jewish scholar are often at curious odds with one another. Of course, in many ways, Meir Kahane perfectly bridged these two extremes and was even known as "The Fighting Rabbi."

In the 1950s, about a decade before he formed The Jewish Defense League, Meir Kahane was a newly married young man beginning to experience the secular world around him in New York. One night, he came upon a small nightclub featuring an up-and-coming Jewish comic. Meir Kahane had heard a little about this comic, so he went in to watch the man's act.

What Kahane saw shocked him to his core. Once on stage, the comic presented himself as physically weak, insecure, and anxious and went so far as to describe these traits as being typical of the American Jew. The man talked about wanting to hide his Jewishness by changing his name, not wanting to date or marry a Jewish girl, and fearing being beaten up by toughs who hated Jews.

Rabbi Kahane had never seen or heard such a portrayal of a Jew *by* a Jew before.

Members of The JDL practice self-defense scenarios

The comic's characterization of the timid, self-loathing Jew came to symbolize how Rabbi Kahane thought of the American Diaspora Jew who had lost all connection to the Warrior spirit of the Bible heroes, of the American Diaspora Jew who had lost all connection to the time when the Jewish People were a self-ruling majority in their own land with their own military.

And so it was with this negative portrayal of the meek Jew with no self-pride in mind that Rabbi Kahane set about reversing how both the world and young Jews perceived the Jewish People; in many ways, The Jewish Defense League was formed as a way to counteract the harmful and inaccurate portrayal Kahane witnessed that evening.

Unlike many minority group members in society, Jews have the advantage of hiding their minority status if they choose by changing their last names or removing their yarmulkes or religious jewelry in public. Rabbi Kahane was extremely opposed to these actions and did not want Jews to try and melt into American society by

giving up their Jewishness out of convenience or
fear. He wanted Jewish People to hold their heads
up high and feel proud of their amazing history.
He actively encouraged members of The JDL to
proudly wear their yarmulkes in public, especially
on those occasions when the public witnessed
them engaging in acts of strength and courage
such as physically protesting neo-Nazis, protecting
Jewish graveyards with weapons in hand, and
patrolling and standing guard outside of
synagogues and Jewish-owned businesses under
threat. Rabbi Kahane and The Jewish Defense
League reclaimed the yarmulke's symbol of
otherness to re-define it as a symbol of
fearlessness.

Members of The JDL practice self-defense scenarios

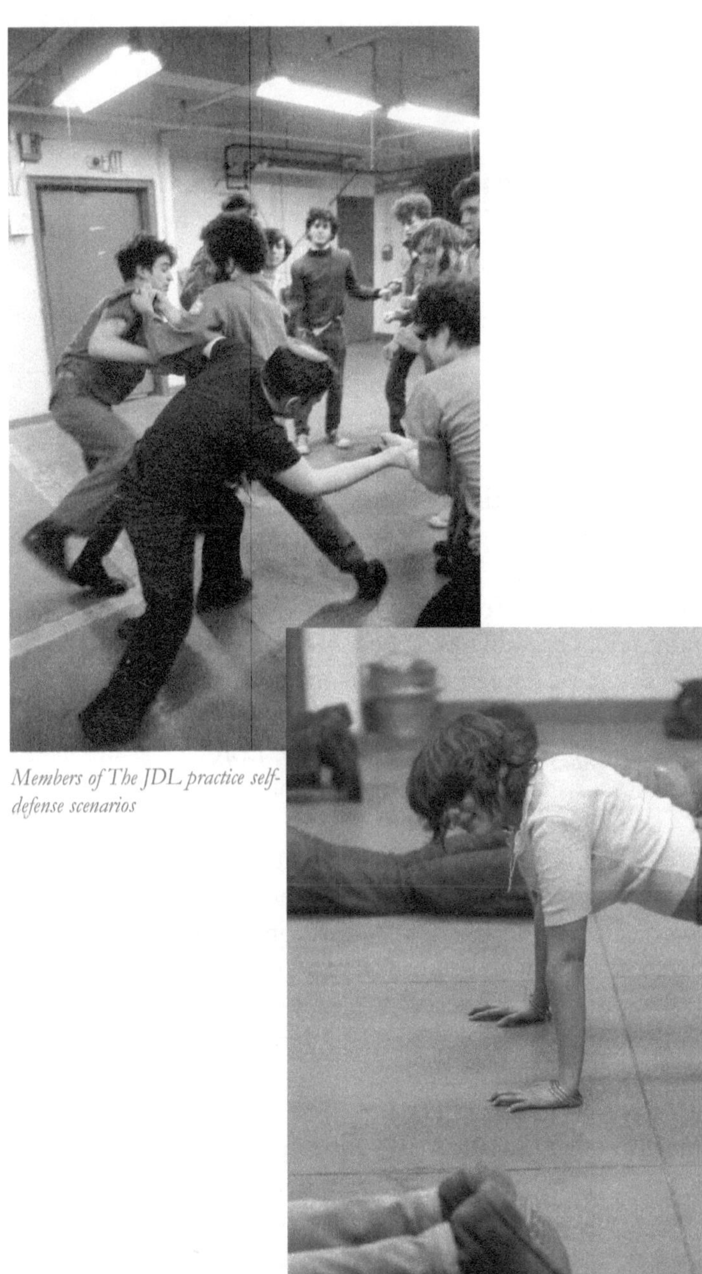

Members of The JDL practice self-defense scenarios

8

JUDAH MACCABEE

"We are not afraid of anything; dead or alive, we are the Children of Israel."

Protest Letter from Soviet Jews, 1968

There was a time when a Hellenistic king named Antiochus ruled over the nation of Judea. His wish was to redesign his nation to mirror Greek society wherein people would give up their defining religion and laws to become one people.

Some of the Jews in the land were willing to obey the king's command and assimilate. Judah, a strong and brave youth faithful to the Lord, refused however, adhering to the Jewish laws even more fervently.

When King Antiochus saw that men like Judah were unwavering in their faith, he decided to put such rebels to death. The king summoned a widowed woman with seven sons and tortured and killed each one as they refused to renounce God. Upon hearing of what had been done to the poor woman's sons, Judah gathered his brothers and cried, "Let's go to Jerusalem and fight for our People and our holy laws!" But **Simon**, Judah's older brother, urged him to be patient as the king's soldiers would soon be coming to their town.

When the soldiers of King Antiochus did indeed come to Modin, they gathered the townspeople in the public square where an altar and an image of Zeus appeared. The officer of the king headed straight for Judah's father, the good priest **Mattathias**, and said, "You are the leader of this town. Come and be the first to bow before my gods and eat the flesh of the sacrificial pig on the altar for all to see and follow."

Mattathias responded boldly to the king's officer in a voice loud enough for all to hear. "My sons and I will not turn away from God and the ways of our fathers!" Just then, an assimilated Jew dressed in Greek clothing stepped to the altar and lifted the knife to make the sacrifice. Mattathias trembled with anger at the sight of this and struck the traitorous man to the ground; he then took the knife and killed the king's officer.

Mattathias' five sons surrounded him as he cried out, "Whoever is for the Lord, follow me!"

Seeking shelter in the nearby caves with other brave men and their families, the brothers hid during the day and ambushed the king's soldiers at night. Judah led many daring and bold attacks against the Syrians, who strove to wipe out the Jewish People, and soon came to be called "Maccabee" as it meant "hard-hitting hammer."

Each day, more Jewish fighters joined Judah and the cause; he came to be known for

Judah Maccabee fought against those who sought to destroy Judaism

having the courage of a lion. Word of Judah and his band of Warriors reached the king who sent his Syrian army to force them out of hiding and destroy them. But Judah did not wait for the Syrians; he brought his band of ragged rebels to the king's forces and – with the Lord's help – destroyed an army 40 times greater than his own.

Rabbi Kahane leads members of The JDL in a celebration of the Maccabees' heroism during Chanukah

9

KAHANE KORNER: JEWS AND THE USE OF PHYSICAL STRENGTH

"To turn the other cheek is indeed in the Bible, but it's not in the Jewish Bible. Sometimes justice takes precedence over peace."

Rabbi Meir Kahane, Founder of The Jewish Defense League

Judah Maccabee was a proud Jew who refused to assimilate and give up his faith. He was a brave Warrior and a fierce fighter who earned the name "hard-hitting hammer." But is being a fighter a Jewish tenet? Is using physical strength against an enemy un-Jewish?

Using violence in self-defense is absolutely not un-Jewish; in fact, the Talmud instructs, "If someone comes to kill you, rise up and kill him first."

When Rabbi Meir Kahane founded The Jewish Defense League in order to protect elderly Jews walking to and from Synagogue from muggings, the media asked the following question: "Is this any way for nice Jewish boys to behave?" In response, Rabbi Kahane took the opportunity to smash the image of the passive Jew and urged his People to get back in touch with the Jews of the Bible who picked up weapons when needed to protect themselves from persecution.

Rabbi Kahane created newspaper ads featuring photos of young, tough Jews holding chains and baseball bats accompanied by the words:

"Is this any way for nice Jewish boys to behave? Maybe, just maybe, nice Jewish boys help pave their own road to Auschwitz."

It was a powerful declaration of the strong new Jew who would never accept victimhood again – and the fact that this new Jew wasn't really new at all, but a logical descendent of the Jewish Warrior of old.

Members of The JDL practicing firearm handling and self-defense techniques

Members of The JDL practicing firearm handling and self-defense techniques

10

MASADA

"Walk tall, walk straight, walk proud, and walk Jewish."

Rabbi Meir Kahane, Founder of The Jewish Defense
League

God did not want the Jewish People to live
as slaves. The Lord wanted us, His Chosen People,
to live as free men and women in the Land He
gave us: Israel.

As such, the Almighty sent Moses to
return to Egypt to demand the release of the
Israelites from slavery so that we would be free
and so that we would serve no other power than
God Himself. Moses led the Exodus of the
Israelites out of Egypt in an act that moved our
People from bondage to freedom, a historical
event that is still celebrated throughout the world
each year at Passover.

And it was on the anniversary of Passover
in 73 A.D. that close to 1,000 brave individuals
chose to die as free men, women, and children
rather than face capture and slavery by pagan
Roman conquerors.

After Judah Maccabee vanquished the
Greeks and ran them out of Israel, the Jewish
People were free for many decades. When the
Romans sought to take away the Jewish People's

religion, freedom, and national independence, the **Great Revolt** and **Jewish-Roman War** began.

As the war raged, a band of daring rebels scaled and took over King Herod's great fortress known as Masada. For three years, courageous freedom fighters – known as **the Zealots** – held back 15,000 Roman troops. Although outnumbered 15 to 1, the Zealots fought valiantly. Eventually, the Romans breached the walls of Masada with battering rams.

Knowing the end was near, Zealot leader **Elazar Ben-Yair** called his People together and urged them to perish as free men and women, saying, "We long ago resolved to serve neither the Romans, nor any other than God Himself. It is still in our power to die bravely, and as free men. Let our wives die unabused, our children without knowledge of slavery."

Like the warriors at Masada, Samson chose to fight and die on his own terms

Before ending their lives, the Jews atop Masada burned the entire hilltop, leaving nothing for the Romans to loot but the food supplies they purposely left intact to show that they had died by choice and not for lack of food.

In the end – faced with the options of being captured, tortured, raped, sold into slavery, or murdered – the Zealots chose to die proudly as Jews with their freedom, religious convictions, and dignity intact.

The harrowing events at Masada have become an eternal symbol of the Jewish fight for freedom, inspiring future uprisings.

11

KAHANE KORNER: REFUSING TO DIE ON

OUR ENEMIES' TERMS

"I would rather die on my feet than live on my knees."

Euripides, Greek Playwright

The theme of refusing to die on our enemies' terms is a common one which ties together the stories of many of our greatest heroes. In the Bible, Samson's mother is instructed by an angel to never cut her son's hair as it is the source of his physical strength. Samson grew up to become the strongest man in the world and single-handedly kept the Israelites safe from the hostile Philistines.

After being bribed by Philistine lords, however, Samson's wife Delilah betrayed him and cut his hair, resulting in Samson losing his strength. Subsequently, he was imprisoned by the Philistines who degraded him by poking out his eyes and chaining him up in public. Samson cried out to the Lord for one last burst of strength so that he could put an end to his humiliation and destroy the enemies of his People in one motion.

Granting his wish, God filled Samson with the power to bring down the columns to which he was bound, allowing Samson to conclude his life with his strength

intact while eliminating his People's tormentors by
the thousands.

The desire to live and die with strength and
dignity on one's own terms is a trait that links our
Bible Warriors and modern Jewish heroes together
for all time. This desire was on full display by the
Zealots atop Masada and by the prisoners who
fought back against their captors during the
Holocaust. Our journey continues...

*Members of The JDL
practicing self-defense
techniques*

Members of The JDL practicing self-defense techniques

12

REAL-LIFE SUPERHEROES: WARRIORS LEADING UP TO AND DURING THE HOLOCAUST

"A time to keep silent and a time to speak up"

Ecclesiastes 3:7, The Holy Bible

At a certain age, all Jewish youth must learn the heartbreaking facts of the planned Nazi genocide of the Jewish People. To realize that there was a group of people who wanted to murder every Jew on the planet can shatter one's innocence and cause a shift in one's perception of the world going forward. Such a revelation can lead one to feel sad, hopeless, and angry, but committed to making sure nothing like that ever happens to the Jewish People again.

The Holocaust was not a sudden event, but one that moved into the lives of its victims gradually, insidiously. Jewish people lost their jobs, homes, and businesses while families were systematically rehomed to ghettos. The radical Nazi party initially asked Jewish families to wear the Star of David to identify them for a short period of time, however, bearing such a symbol became commonplace and the law. Jewish children could no longer attend schools and Jewish businesses were looted and burned to the ground. Jews were attacked and killed in the streets. Observant Jews and rabbis were humiliated and degraded by Nazi soldiers who cut off their beards in public. Jews were stripped of all of their rights as citizens and human beings.

During the Holocaust, Jews were packed to capacity into cattle cars with no water, food, bathroom facilities, or ventilation. Their heads were shaved and they were stripped naked. Gold fillings were violently yanked from their mouths. Children were taken from their mothers' arms. Jews were hung, electrocuted, gassed in showers, starved, experimented on, shot, decapitated, and burned in ovens.

But not all went compliantly to their deaths; some actually fought back against their tormentors. Events such as the Warsaw Ghetto Uprising have been well-documented, while others, like the remarkable case of ballerina **Franceska Mann**, are lesser known but incredibly powerful.

In 1943, a convoy of 1,700 Polish Jews arrived at the concentration camp at Auschwitz. All of the women, including the beautiful dancer Franceska Mann, were sent to the gas chambers where they were told to remove their clothes. Noticing that the German guards were paying special attention to her based on her looks and celebrity, Mann lured them closer by undressing provocatively. One Nazi guard came close enough to Mann that she was able to punch him in the face and grab his gun; she then shot him in the stomach. As a second Nazi soldier charged her, Franceska Mann shot and killed him. Witnessing the bravery and resolve of this slight ballerina, other Jewish women sprang into action and attacked the remaining

Nazis with their fists. Refusing to be led to the slaughter like sheep, these heroic women died on their feet with their strength and dignity intact.

During World War II, thousands of Jewish-Americans enthusiastically signed up to join the military to defeat an enemy that sought to wipe the entirety of their People off of the face of the earth. In 1944, the most ambitious operation of the war, known as D-Day, was planned and, despite rough weather and uncertainties, implemented. On June 6, 1944, more than 160,000 men invaded occupied France from the sea. These soldiers faced the most dangerous battle of the war, having little to no cover to protect them from enemy machine-gun fire; indeed, two out of every three soldiers experienced almost immediate death on some of the more hard-hit beaches.

Jewish-American soldier **Harold "Hal" Baumgarten** was there that day amongst just 30 other soldiers in his unit who had survived the enemy onslaught of gunfire. The only Jew in his unit, Baumgarten joined the other men as they hid behind two tanks to avoid certain death. Looking at his fellow soldiers and knowing that the enemy sought to weaken, degrade, and treat the Jewish People like pathetic and powerless animals, Hal Baumgarten felt a surge of power and conviction overcome him. He took his army field jacket off, drew a giant Star of David on the garment, then put the jacket back on and grabbed his gun. Rushing fearlessly toward the seawall without cover, Baumgarten survived and engaged in gunfire with the Nazis – all the while, displaying the giant Star of David on his uniform for all to see how courageous and proud a Jew could be in the most perilous of situations.

As we examine Jewish Warriors from the time of the Bible to the present day, it is important to put everything into the context of self-defense and survival. The Sixth Commandment, in its original Hebrew, does not say "Thou Shalt Not Kill;" rather, it says "Thou Shalt Not Murder." If the Sixth Commandment forbade us to kill under any circumstance, God would command us to be pacifists. The true wording of the Commandment makes it clear that there is such a thing as a moral killing – most obviously when used in self-defense against a murderous aggressor.

The pages of Jewish history are filled with incredibly daring individuals who fought all odds to maintain their dignity, religious faith, strength, and sense of humanity even during the darkest of times. Let us shed light on real-life Warriors leading up to and during the Holocaust and the ways in which they shaped the course of Jewish history with their fearlessness and devotion to God.

13

ZE'EV JABOTINSKY

"Jews, get moving. There is no time. A fire is burning, get out."

Ze'ev Jabotinsky, Zionist Activist

Ze'ev Jabotinsky (pronounced "Jah–Bo–TIN–skee") was an orator, writer, political thinker, and soldier who desired precisely three things for the Jewish People:

(1) the entirety of the Land that God promised the Jews in the Bible;

(2) for the Jews to be trained and ready to defend themselves against any enemy;

(3) and for the Jews of Europe to immigrate to Israel immediately.

Like a Jewish Paul Revere, Ze'ev Jabotinsky rode through Europe to alert his People to the dangers that swelled all around them. Knowing that history was filled with endless examples of the Jewish People being targeted, scapegoated, and attacked, Jabotinsky beseeched his fellow Jews to not be the only vulnerable minority group in the world unable to operate firearms.

Following violent attacks against Jews and the destruction of their homes and businesses in Russia in 1903, Ze'ev Jabotinsky fervently sought to re-establish a Jewish homeland in Israel for his

People's safety. Seeing Jews attacked and degraded spurred Jabotinsky to travel throughout Russia, urging his People to learn self-defense. Jabotinsky was especially active between 1917 and 1937, a time that saw great upheaval around the world and, of course, the rise of Nazi Germany. He served as a lieutenant and participated in the assault to free Israel from oppressive Turkish rule.

As the head of the **Haganah** (an underground military organization in Israel), Jabotinsky stood against violent Arab riots which targeted the Jewish People. He led the **Betar Movement** aimed at instilling young Jews with a militaristic and nationalistic spirit and filling their souls with the drive to liberate and re-establish Israel. As the commander of **Etzel**, he led a military arm that fought against the enemies of Zionism. From 1939 to 1940, Ze'ev Jabotinsky worked to establish a Jewish army to fight side-by-side with Britain and the United States against Adolph Hitler and Nazi Germany.

In 1940, Ze'ev Jabotinsky came to Brooklyn, New York to meet with his supporters in the home of Rabbi Yechezkel Kahane, father of Meir Kahane, who

Ze'ev Jabotinsky beseeched the Jewish People to wake up to the impending Holocaust and to learn to defend themselves

was a young boy at the time. Introducing his young son to

Ze'ev Jabotinsky, Yechezkel could hardly have
known that Meir would grow up to be the spiritual
successor to the great activist and that the simple
handshake that transpired between them would
become such a symbolic gesture of the passing of
the torch from one great Jewish Warrior and
Protector to another.

14

KAHANE KORNER: RABBI KAHANE ON

ZE'EV JABOTINSKY

"Don't be the only people in this world - you, the most hated of peoples - who can't handle weapons."

Ze'ev Jabotinsky, Zionist Activist

Ze'ev Jabotinsky urged the Jewish People to learn to defend themselves, exhorting them to wake up to the approaching threat of Adolph Hitler. He implored the Jewish People to re-connect with their history of powerful kings, mighty armies, and self-determination. He compelled the Jewish People to take pride in the royal and Warrior blood that still flows in our veins.

Excerpt from E.A. Schwartz/Meir Kahane Interview New York, January 1975

E.A. SCHWARTZ: I want to go way back in history. I've been reading and studying a little bit and people have told me about Ze'ev Jabotinsky, who seems to be a key figure in the development of this whole line of thinking that led to The JDL. Can you tell me about Ze'ev Jabotinsky?

RABBI MEIR KAHANE: Ze'ev Jabotinsky was probably the first person to start turning back the clock of The

57

Exile. Once upon a time, Jews lived in their own land and had a pride and had an army who fought and were a majority. And they have lost not only their majority and their land, but everything else that went with it. And Jabotinsky was undoubtedly the first man in 2,000 years who began to turn the clock back and spoke of pride and Jewish strength. And because of that, I think that he has become the father of the whole ideology. There is no question that his writings and his thinking play a great part in my own personal thinking and, of course, in JDL.

EAS: When was he active?

RMK: Jabotinsky was born in 1880 and he was instrumental in creating the first Jewish fighting force since the Jews went into exile. He preached throughout the twenties and thirties the fact that the official aim of Zionism should be a Jewish state. Jabotinsky was also, of course, the first one to see the approaching Holocaust in the 1930s. And he warned – he wrote over and over again – he warned the Jews of the impending Holocaust. And he pleaded with them to leave Europe. He also attempted to train Jews in Europe in self-defense. He called upon them to learn how to shoot. He died in 1940 here in America. Jabotinsky was in our home, though I don't remember him. I was only five or six. My father says that I shook hands with him. Jabotinsky was a tremendous Jewish hero. Tremendous hero.

15

SOBIBOR CONCENTRATION CAMP

"The lesson from the Holocaust is that we must be able to defend ourselves by ourselves against all threats and against any enemy."

Benjamin Netanyahu, Israeli Prime Minister

In the late 1930s, Adolph Hitler and the Nazis began rounding up the Jews and shipping them to death camps. Crammed to capacity into windowless cattle wagons, Jews were shipped to concentration camps where family members were forcibly separated from each other upon arrival. Every single Jew was marked for death; the old, the young, and the sick were exterminated immediately while everyone else was assigned slave labor until their certain death.

One such death camp was called Sobibor. Located in Poland, Sobibor was like all of the other extermination camps; it was permeated with exhaustion, desperation, degradation, starvation, cruelty, death, and cremation. It was also filled with Nazi guards armed with machine guns. Despite the insurmountable odds of success, the Jews of the Sobibor death camp attempted a revolt against their evil captors.

Led by three valiant Jewish Warriors – **Leon Feldhendler, Shlomo Leitman,** and **Alexander "Sasha" Pechersky** – the prisoners realized that their only chance at survival was to take action and try to liberate themselves. If their survival was not to be, then these

plucky Jews hoped to at least go down fighting –
to defiantly die as proud Jews – and to kill as many
of their oppressors along the way as possible to
prevent them from torturing and murdering more
Jews in the future.

The prisoners' plan revolved around the
carpentry, tailoring, and shoemaking workshops in
the camp where they were forced to manufacture
Nazi boots and leather coats; whilst unsupervised,
the prisoners began to make knives and hatchets
for their secret revolt.

Since the Nazis adhered to highly
systematic daily routines, the Jewish prisoners were
able to plan their attacks on the guards to the
minute as to when they would arrive at the
different workshops. One by one, as the guards
checked in at the various locations, Jewish
prisoners armed with primitive weapons
bludgeoned and stabbed their oppressors and took
their guns.

As the 600 Jewish men and women were
fleeing the death camp, Alexander "Sasha"
Pechersky stood up and addressed his People:
"Our day has come. Let's die with honor.
Remember, if anyone survives, he must tell the
world what has happened here!"

At that, a stampede of Jewish feet made its
way past gates, through fences, across minefields,
and into the waiting arms of the forest. Hundreds
of them survived, many joining other bold men,
women, and teenagers to form armed
"Resistance" fighter groups against the Nazis.

16

JEWISH RESISTANCE FIGHTERS

"We wanted to create a Jew who would teach the world that 'Jew' was not a synonym for 'victim.'"

Rabbi Meir Kahane, Founder of The Jewish Defense League

Jewish Resistance Fighters, sometimes known as **'Partisans,'** fought against the Nazis in nearly every country in Europe during the Holocaust. Close to 30,000 Jewish men, women, and teenagers escaped ghettos and concentration camps to bravely battle their evil enemies through force.

Hiding primarily in the forests and mountains, these lionhearted Jews operated primarily under the cover of darkness to sabotage the murderous plans of the Nazis. They disabled trains to be used for shipping Jewish victims to the gas chambers, planted dynamite on railway tracks, and blew up thousands of transportation systems carrying weapons for Nazi use. They also destroyed a multitude of Nazi power plants and factories.

Those individuals who had previous military training taught the others to properly handle guns and ammunition. Compared to the Nazis, the Jewish Resistance Fighters had few guns and little ammunition - but what they lacked in weaponry, they made up for in their knowledge of the local terrain which they used to their advantage when Nazis would enter the forest.

The Nazis sought not only to kill their Jewish victims but to take away their dignity and self-respect while they were alive. The Jewish Resistance Fighters were determined to stand tall and fight back against their tormentors and did so with immense bravery. They were heroes who stood up for themselves and for their People in the Maccabee spirit.

17

KAHANE KORNER: THE JEWISH WARRIOR AND SELF-CONTROL

"Who is strong? He who conquers desire."

Rabbi Meir Kahane, Founder of The Jewish Defense League

Jewish Resistance Fighters, sometimes known as 'Partisans,' engaged in successful guerilla warfare and sabotage against the murderous Nazis. They lent life-saving resources and assistance to fellow Jews trapped in ghettos and concentration camps and shared vital strategic information with other resistance groups. These Resistance Fighters accomplished all they did with nothing more than the disintegrating clothes on their backs, teetering on the edge of starvation and sleeping in makeshift shallow pits in the ground.

The Resistance Fighters sought to get supplies to fellow Jews even though they themselves had no possessions. They worked to deliver food to fellow Jews even though they themselves were close to starving. The discipline, self-control, and mental and physical strength required of the Resistance Fighters to help their fellow Jews when the Resistance Fighters could barely help themselves is astounding.

Many of these Jewish Warriors had grown up in observant homes where laws, commandments, discipline, and self-control were prized values and vital preparation for becoming future Resistance Fighters; much of that self-control was instilled through the observance of the Sabbath.

God commands us to observe the Sabbath and to keep it holy by abstaining from working, creating, and all possibilities of monetary gain; this means we are to remove all creation and materialism from our hands and minds and focus on the Lord while acknowledging our miniscule role within the universe. On this day, we remember that our material prosperity is, in fact, the handiwork of God so we relinquish our materialistic desires and avoid the physical.

Proud members of The Jewish Defense League

As we master the ability to sacrifice and to do without, we acquire the strength of will and discipline. Likewise, the mitzvot of following dietary Kosher laws helps to build great resolve and character within Jewish Warriors of all ages.

To illustrate this point, Rabbi Kahane loved to share the story of the Kosher-observant youth with a ticket to a baseball game. In the example, this young person attends a double-header that goes into extra innings and is now extremely hungry. This Jewish youth sits through the entire game while one delicious-smelling hot dog after another is passed down the row. Famished but refusing to order a hot dog, this young person experiences a tremendous thing: a realization of the capacity to do without if necessary. Subsequently, the youth discovers the inner ability and resolve to resist what is desperately desired.

Over time, such exercises in self-control allow the Jewish Warrior to build up the necessary strength to face any sacrifice required for the survival of self, family, or Tribe. Observing these laws connects us to our lineage of self-command while bringing us closer to holiness.

A proud member of The JDL

18

THE WARSAW GHETTO UPRISING

"The Warsaw Resistance - when the Jews finally did fight back - is one of the most glorious chapters in Jewish history."

Irv Rubin, National Chairman of The Jewish Defense League

Nazi Germany (1933-1943) was systematic in its plan to entirely cleanse the world of the Jewish People. After being forced to surrender their guns, jobs, homes, businesses, and human rights, hundreds of thousands of Jewish men, women, and children were sent to large walled-in slums called ghettos. These filthy, barricaded spaces were used as transitional measures wherein Jews were separated from general society, ostracized, and marked in preparation to be shipped off to extermination camps. Ghettos were dangerously overcrowded and disease-ridden. Food was extremely scarce and Jews of all ages scattered the grounds like starving skeletons.

By 1943, nearly half a million Jews were struggling to survive in a ghetto in Warsaw, Poland. For almost three years, they had clung to life in this ghetto by secretly negotiating with smugglers to bring in food supplies. Mystified and angered by the Warsaw Jews' determination and ability to survive their grim predicament, the Nazis decided to raze the ghetto and its residents; the timing of the destruction was cruelly chosen to coincide with both Passover and Adolph Hitler's birthday.

After word of this plan got out in the ghetto via underground communications, some 750 Jewish men, women, and teenagers came together to form a self-defense unit. Led by 24-year-old **Mordechai Anielewicz**, the group acquired pistols, grenades, automatic weapons, and rifles through their smuggler contacts.

As the German forces entered the ghetto to begin their attack, they were met by an army of fierce Jewish fighters. For 28 days, gun battles ensued with many Nazis dying at the hands of a people they believed to be weak and genetically inferior.

In the final days of the Warsaw Ghetto Uprising, the Nazis used their access to tanks and flamethrowers to overpower the Jewish Warriors ; the site was ultimately reduced to rubble. Still, a small group of determined Jews had accomplished the unthinkable: they had gone head-to-head with an organized military entity and inflicted mass damage for over a month.

The Jewish heroes of the Warsaw Ghetto Uprising stood together as one People with an unwavering will to survive.

The Jewish heroes of the Warsaw Ghetto Uprising stood together to reject death on the Nazis' terms.

19

REAL-LIFE SUPERHEROES: IN THE AFTERMATH OF THE HOLOCAUST

"Never again will the anti-Semite be able to exterminate the Jew and never again will the Jew be an 'easy mark' for anti-Semites."

Janet L. Dolgin, Writer/Anthropologist

Some say Israel only exists because of the Holocaust.

That is incorrect.

There was a Holocaust because Israel didn't exist.

Prime Minister of Israel **Golda Meir** once wisely remarked, "Israel itself is the strongest guarantee against another Holocaust."

In 132 C.E., a large Roman presence in Judea attempted to take over and control the territory, political decisions, and sacred prayer sites of the indigenous Jewish People. The ultimate goal was to prohibit Torah law, nullify the Hebrew calendar, and erase the Jewish identity of Judea. In response, a Jewish rebellion against the Roman Empire took place under the leadership of Commander **Simon bar Kokhba**.

Initially succeeding against the enormous Roman army, the daring **"Bar Kokhba Revolt"** managed to inflict heavy casualties on the Romans through the use of guerilla warfare; after three years, however, the Romans completely crushed the uprising with over half a million Jews tortured and murdered following their defeat. The sacred scrolls of Judaism were burned on the Temple Mount and the Jewish People were expelled from their God-given Homeland. Known as the Diaspora, the Jewish People were thus scattered to the corners of the world to live as vulnerable strangers in strange lands without a true home or army of their own.

The Romans changed the name of Judea to "Palestine" as a final insult to the Jews and in an effort to fool the world into forgetting the Jewish connection to the land. Amazingly, a small population of Jews remained in the territory, meaning that there has never been a period in the many thousands of years of Israel's history without a Jewish presence.

Violence, victimization, pogroms, and the Holocaust occurred because the Jewish People were now the ultimate outsiders at the mercy of a non-Jewish world. Following the Holocaust in which six million of our People were murdered, a myriad of heroic Jewish men and women worked in various ways to make the dream of a homeland-reborn a reality.

Never Again would we be denied our God-given, ancestral Home.

Never Again would we lack a safe place to return should a future attempt to wholly eliminate us be put into action.

Never Again would we be defenseless, unarmed, and without a mighty army to protect ourselves.

Never Again would every People in the world have a right
to self-governance and a Land of their own but the Jews.

Let us examine some real-life superheroes
following the Holocaust who contributed to the
rebirth of Israel as the eternal Jewish Homeland,
the rebirth of Jewish strength and pride, and the
rebirth of the Zionist spirit.

We salute them all as each helped to shape
the course of Jewish history with their bravery and
devotion to God.

20

NAZI HUNTERS

"When history looks back, I want people to know the Nazis weren't able to kill millions of people and get away with it."

Simon Wiesenthal, Holocaust Survivor and Nazi Hunter

Four years after the war ended to stop Adolph Hitler, only 300 of the 13 million Nazis who had taken part in the torture and murder of Jews were in prison. At the famous Nuremberg Trials, just 24 individuals were called to account for the greatest crimes in human history.

Had the Nazis lost the war but gotten away with murder? Did the allies have the patience and fortitude to try and jail essentially the entire male population of Germany? The war was over and, after a tiny percentage of Nazis were symbolically prosecuted, it seemed the world was anxious to move on.

But what about the survivors of the Holocaust? They had lived through starvation, torture, degradation, the murder of loved ones and children, and the loss of their homes and businesses – were *they* ready to move on? Many were not. As such, they valiantly devoted their lives to the pursuit of justice and to avenging the blood of their fellow Jews.

One such hero was **Simon Wiesenthal**, a Holocaust survivor who aggressively sought to hunt down and prosecute Nazis who had evaded justice throughout the world. Wiesenthal's efforts led to the capture, extradition, and trials of Nazis ranging from the highest-ranking architects of Hitler's genocidal plan down to lower-ranking prison guards who hid in plain sight as unassuming housewives after the war.

In 1945, a group of Holocaust survivors came together at a Passover service in Bucharest to recite Psalm 94, which focuses on the manner in which The Almighty promises to deal with the enemies of Israel: "He will repay them for their iniquity and wipe them out for their wickedness." Led by **Abba Kovner**, the head of a ghetto Uprising in the Baltics during the Holocaust, this group of survivors resolved to form '**The Novkim**' – Hebrew for "**The Avengers**," deciding amongst themselves that if the courts of international justice would not hold former Nazis accountable for their deeds, then the Jews would do it themselves. The Avengers doggedly scoured the globe, tracking down Nazi war criminals and bringing them to justice through a series of daring scenarios on par with Hollywood's greatest action movies and spy dramas.

The message to future generations was clear: the world could no longer bully, degrade, and murder Jews with impunity. Jewish defense groups of the 1960s hammered this point home with a vengeance.

21

KAHANE KORNER: VIGILANTISM

"The saddest thing about those who condemn violence is usually their own distance from personal danger."

Rabbi Meir Kahane, Founder of The Jewish Defense League

Rabbi Meir Kahane felt a love and connection to all Jewish People, but none more acutely perhaps than elderly Jews struggling to survive in poverty-stricken, crime-ridden neighborhoods; in fact, The Jewish Defense League came into existence as a result of the Rabbi's awareness that elderly Holocaust survivors were being mugged at night whilst walking home from Synagogue.

When the police in these areas were either unable or unwilling to protect these frail victims, Rabbi Kahane and The Jewish Defense League set up 'self-defense patrols' consisting of Jews on foot and in automobiles. Armed with two-way radios and legally licensed weapons, these individuals patrolled both buildings and streets in order to protect the most vulnerable of our Tribe.

Familiar with the codes pertaining to a citizen's right to apprehend criminals, the members of these patrols would inform the police by radio when a crime was being committed. If captured, the members of the patrol would detain the criminal(s) until the arrival of the police. Often, the mere presence of Jewish toughs standing guard in front of Synagogues and Jewish businesses with pipes and baseball bats was enough of a deterrent to cause anti-Semites to move on without incident.

Based on these actions, some accused The JDL and other Jewish defense groups of being vigilantes. Scoffing at this charge, Rabbi Kahane

Self-defense patrols organized by The Jewish Defense League

argued that vigilantism, by definition, only exists when an individual takes the law into his or her own hands *despite* the fact that there is adequate law enforcement. In the cases of elderly Jews being mugged on the way home from Synagogue or being robbed and targeted whilst running their businesses, the police proved themselves lacking in staff size and effort.

Rabbi Kahane and The JDL ensured that one way or another, these forgotten Jews in dangerous neighborhoods would be protected. When the police informed Rabbi Kahane that they did not have enough men to handle the problem, the Rabbi responded defiantly, "Well, *we* do."

Members of The JDL taking their message to the streets

22

MENACHEM BEGIN

"Eretz Israel will be restored to the People of Israel. All of it. And forever."

Menachem Begin, Commander of The Irgun

When the Romans conquered Israel, many hundreds of thousands of Jews were either deported, sold as slaves, or killed. The Romans renamed the land "Palestine" in an attempt to eliminate any Jewish connection to the region. In the subsequent centuries, control over Israel changed hands, bouncing between the Persians, Arabs, European Crusaders, and Ottoman Turks, before finally settling with the British. In 1917, the "Balfour Declaration" was issued, announcing world support for the Land of Israel to finally be returned to its indigenous rightful owners – the Jewish People.

Five years later, the League of Nations unanimously voted to create the conditions for the re-establishment of a national home for the Jewish People, leading the Balfour Document to become accepted by all of the united nations. From that point on, however, progress was slow on the part of the British to make the rebirth of Israel a reality; in actuality, it would be another 25 more years before the state of Israel was re-established.

During those years, Britain attempted to retain its rule, seeking to impede the mass immigration of Jews, including desperate Holocaust survivors, into Israel while prohibiting the sale and purchase of land to Jews. Britain broke promises and changed policies on how territories were to be divided, eventually leading many Jews to abandon hope that a Jewish state would ever again exist.

It was during this tumultuous time that an underground Zionist paramilitary organization called **The Irgun** was formed. Led by a rowdy young man with a fiery personality, Menachem Begin (pronounced Muh-NOK-Um BAY-ghin), The Irgun maintained that any action taken in the cause of the re-establishment of a Jewish state was justified and that, in fact, *only* armed force would ensure a Jewish state.

Menachem Begin had joined Ze'ev Jabotinsky's Betar youth movement in his teens. Through his experiences in Betar, Begin had learned well the history of his People and carried in his heart the

Menachem Begin used force and determination to ensure the re-establishment of a Jewish state

truths surrounding the fact that Jews descended from kings and princes. He knew that the blood of heroes such as King David, Samson, and Judah Maccabee ran through the veins of all indigenous People of Israel. Like Jabotinsky, Begin believed that the Jewish People needed to be unified in the pursuit of a Jewish state that once was ours and to which our claim had never expired.

In preparation to resist the British, members of The Irgun trained with firearms and hand grenades. Strict drill exercises were carried out with an emphasis on efficiency and discipline. In 1944, The Irgun officially proclaimed a revolt against the occupying British government in Israel. Attacks were carried out on immigration offices, railroads, communication lines, and bridges. In all cases, The Irgun provided advanced warning so that all civilians could avoid being harmed.

The ensuing violence succeeded in bringing international attention to the situation. And with the whole world watching, a public relations nightmare came to a head when the British refused to allow a ship carrying nearly 5,000 Holocaust survivors to enter what should have been the safe haven of a Jewish homeland. Britain's disgraceful actions drew widespread condemnation and caused them international embarrassment. The Irgun succeeded in defeating the British through both physical force and by swaying the court of public opinion. Just two weeks later, Menachem Begin and The Irgun emerged victorious in their efforts when the House of Commons voted to withdraw all British soldiers from the area; the ancient Jewish homeland was finally returned to those whom God had chosen.

On May 14, 1948, the re-establishment of the State of Israel was proclaimed and the mighty forces of The Irgun were absorbed into the newly established Israel Defense Forces (IDF). While Zionist leaders and visionaries such as **David Ben-Gurion** and **Theodor Herzl** provided important political and philosophical skills toward the re-establishment of a Jewish state, the Irgun brought the required muscle and Warrior spirit to the endeavor.

In 1977, Menachem Begin was elected Prime Minister of Israel.

23

ZIONISM: THE BELIEF THAT ISRAEL HAS THE RIGHT TO EXIST

"Zionism is the Civil Rights Movement of the Jewish People."

Herut North America

Interview with Lauren Isaacs, Toronto Director of Herut Canada
Israel, March 2020

Unapologetic Zionist Lauren Isaacs, Toronto Director of Herut Canada

Above & subsequent photos courtesy of Herut North America

ROSS BERG: Can you give us a brief explanation of the goals of Herut Canada and what a typical day might look like for you as an advocate for Jewish pride and the righteousness of Israel?

LAUREN ISAACS: Herut Canada is an unapologetically Zionist organization. We promote and educate true Zionism. We run talks, seminars, and speak in high schools and universities all the time, educating about the

Jewish People's rights to the ancient homeland (*Eretz Yisrael*), Jerusalem as the eternal capital of Israel, and *Aliyah* as a practical step for Zionists. We want to engage people with their Zionist identities and take the narrative back. No longer should we remain silent… We are loud and proud Zionists!

RB: Do you feel that anti-Zionism is akin to anti-Semitism? Please explain.

LI: Anti-Zionism and anti-Semitism are one and the same. Zionism is simply the Jewish People's right to live freely in their homeland – to self-determine. To deny the Jews this right of self-determination (while all other people are afforded this right) is pure anti-Semitism. To deny someone something so fundamental to their identity and existence is egregious. There is no difference between anti-Zionism and anti-Semitism.

Lauren Isaacs educating college students about Israel

RB: Rabbi Meir Kahane, Founder of The Jewish Defense League, often visited college campuses in order to connect with Jewish youth. He was routinely shocked to see Jewish dorm rooms decorated with posters of revolutionaries such as Malcolm X and Che Guevara rather than Jewish heroes like Ze'ev Jabotinsky and Menachem Begin. How do we do a better job of bringing awareness to our Jewish youth of the countless brave Warriors and heroes that constitute Jewish history?

LI: This all starts with education, both at school and at home. We need to be raising our children with the stories of their history and the great history of Israel. Children should look to Golda Meir, Menachem Begin, and many others who founded and built the State of Israel. These are not only heroes but they are the foundational characters in our Jewish and Zionist history. This information should be taught more regularly in schools, but if it is not, it has always been (and will always be) our duty to educate ourselves and the future generations.

RB: For critics of organizations such as The Jewish Defense League, there seems to be an assertion that violence is un-Jewish. What do you say about this?

LI: I can only speak for myself and my organization, but we do not condone violence unless it is in the case of self-defense. We should strive to solve conflicts peacefully, using logic and dialogue. With regard to defending ourselves, we have every right to do so. This is why I, along with so many others, support the Israel Defense Forces (IDF) with my whole heart. They are there solely to protect the Jewish people and the Jewish state. This is vital to our survival. With Israel, Jews are no longer unable to defend themselves. This is a positive thing!

RB: Why is the existence of Israel so important?

LI: Israel is our eternal homeland and Holy Land for the Jewish People. Without Israel, we are perpetually in a state of exile. Without Israel, we have no home or religious center. Besides the biblical, religious, and historical connections between the Jewish people and the land, Israel is strategically vital in Jewish survival. The IDF and Israel defend and protect Jews all over the world, ensuring that massacres such as the Holocaust don't happen again. Without Israel, we are a defenseless, exiled people with no land. The country is imperative to our physical protection and for our Biblical [and]religious goals. Judaism and Israel go hand-in-hand. We must always protect our Homeland.

RB: From your experiences tabling on college campuses and in your speaking engagements, what is the most common false belief expressed by haters of Israel and how do you respond to their charges?

LI: The most common false accusation made by students is that Israel is killing Palestinians and committing a mass genocide. This is patently false and easily disprovable, though that doesn't stop people from repeating the lie. Haters of Israel and anti-Semites repeat this false accusation because it supports their narrative, it justifies their desire to steal and own the entire land of Israel, and it justifies violence against Jews. Population numbers alone disprove this claim, although it is difficult to fight with facts when the other side fights with fiction.

RB: Was there a 'lightning bolt' moment or event in your life that led you to become such a fearless advocate for Jews and for Israel?

LI: I visited Israel for the first time when I was 20 years old and I absolutely fell in love with the country. I saw first-hand why Israel is so magnificent and how She makes the Middle East (and the world) a much better place. I also began connecting to my Jewish identity more at that time, and naturally, this means connecting to Zionism more.

I've never been a quiet person, and when I feel passionately about something, I say it loud and proud. Israel is our home as Jews, and it is a wonderful country. We should all be standing with Israel and doing what we can to defend our Homeland.

Isaacs presenting on "Countering Antisemitism"

RB: Is there a Jewish hero or warrior that you particularly admire? If so, who would that be and why?

LI: There are too many wonderful people to name just one, but I sincerely admire Golda Meir, Menachem Begin, and Ze'ev Jabotinsky. Golda Meir demonstrated immense strength and love of country, while maintaining a wonderful attitude and outlook. She was a strong and fierce Zionist. I will also say that I admire Abraham as a Biblical hero. He left his land and was led, with full trust in

God, to the unknown Promised Land. This is an attribute
we should all strive to embody as Zionists.

RB: How can we best prepare our Jewish youth for the
anti-Israel rhetoric and demonstrations they will surely
encounter upon arriving on today's college campuses?

LI: We must teach them about the lies they will hear and
the truth that must counter it. In order for them to know
how to defend Israel on campus, they must be educated in
all the facts. We must also impress upon them the
importance of caring about Israel at all – why they should
care and historically what happens if they don't. It is also
important to connect Jews with their Jewish identity. This
helps to foster a love and understanding of true Zionism.
Education, asking and answering questions, reading books,
Jewish identity, and constantly speaking about the issues
are all important here.

RB: Thank you so much for your time, Lauren. Is there
anything else you would like to add?

LI: Thank you so much for your questions. I will end off
by saying that Zionism is a moral, ethical, civil rights
movement and a foundation of Judaism. We must all
strive to be proud, educated, and knowledgeable Zionists.
We must also continue to educate the next generation
about the importance of the Land of Israel and our eternal
connection to it. There is no shame in Zionism… There is
only immense pride.

24

KAHANE KORNER: JEWS AND THE IMPORTANCE OF ISRAEL

"You cannot support Jews and be against Israel, for Israel is part of the Jewish People from Abraham until today. It lives in our culture, it flows in our blood, it soars in our spirit. If you're against Israel, then you're against the very first Jew that ever existed."

Justin Amler, Jewish Journalist, 'Israelly Cool'

The State of Israel is a decree. It is an obligation, a Jewish commandment. Rabbinic teachings instruct us that living in Israel is equal to all of the commandments of the Torah. Rabbi Meir Kahane urged the Jewish People to return to Zion where they could live as a majority with Jewish sovereignty in their own Land. And that Land is promised and God-given.

For the entire world to see the Jewish People taking their rightful place in the Promised Land is to sanctify the name of the Lord, God of Israel. Conversely, when the Jewish People are in exile as beaten strangers in foreign lands, the Lord's name is desecrated as the non-Jew mocks, "If the God of Israel truly exists, why would His chosen People be living in exile? If it's so easy to humiliate and destroy the Jew, then perhaps his God is impotent or even non-existent."

By returning to the Land God chose for us, building a world-class military, creating an oasis of freedom and democracy within an otherwise dark corner of the world, and thriving as a majority in a Homeland that is uniquely our own, we make His greatness and omnipotence abundantly clear to all nations of the world.

The rebirth of the State of Israel is proof of the hand of God.

Members of The JDL proudly flying the flag of Israel

Rabbi Kahane speaking to members of The JDL about the God-given Land of Israel

*Members of The JDL proudly
flying the flag of Israel*

25

MEIR KAHANE AND THE JEWISH DEFENSE LEAGUE

"Rabbi Meir Kahane is a really sincere guy - a nice, patient teacher. He's really put it all together."

Bob Dylan, Pulitzer Prize-Winning Jewish-American Songwriter

Jewish Defense League Leader Fern Sidman Recalls Rabbi Kahane and the Origins of The JDL

Fern Sidman is a Journalist and Jewish Warrior whose history includes active membership in the Betar Youth Movement and in The Jewish Defense League.

The Jewish Defense League was established in 1968 in the aftermath of the Ocean Hill-Brownsville inspired teachers' strike. At the time, a large percentage of New York City (NYC) public school teachers were Jewish. Subsequently, anti-Semitic organizations began claiming that Jews dominated the school system and were somehow controlling the curriculum and destiny of all students. This was patently false but, as a result, a tremendous wave of anti-Semitism erupted to target Jewish teachers, principals, and administrators with the hope of pushing them out of the educational system. It was, for the most part, successful.

Anti-Semitism spread like wildfire in the days during and after the 1968 teachers' strike. In addition to the harsh criticism that Jewish teachers suffered, physical attacks on poor Jews living in certain changing neighborhoods in New York City were commonplace. The Jewish Defense League immediately sought to change that by training young Jews to fight back as they organized street patrols to help beleaguered Jews who could not get adequate protection from the police.

The JDL **Chaya Squad** ("Animal Squad") which comprised of young Jewish boys and men who were trained in street fighting, martial arts, and investigative procedures, was formed. Young Jews were also offered firearms training and the famous Kahane slogan "Every Jew, a .22" was established.

In addition to changing the course of history through championing such issues as the freedom of Soviet Jews and fighting to defend Israel, The JDL was in the forefront of combatting the ever-increasing rate of anti-Semitism. The JDL became known as the go-to organization who would patrol Jewish cemeteries that had been vandalized, and would defend Yeshiva (school for Talmudic studies) students who had been harassed, bullied and attacked. The JDL would provide escorts for elderly Jews who could not afford to flee the city for the safer suburbs and were often prey for young anti-Semites who attacked their homes and properties and viciously beat and mugged them on a frequent basis.

We should be reminded that the late-1960s and early-1970s was an era that was rife with political activism and defined by historians as intrinsically turbulent. The civil rights movement gained formidable momentum while anti-war sentiments swelled in response to the miserable

handling of the Vietnam War. Young people of all
stripes were in a state of rebellion against
established practices and traditional institutions.
Every group called for its rights to be heard and
addressed as they employed militant tactics in
expressions of outrage and consternation. The
women's rights movement emerged alongside gay
rights demonstrations and migrant workers' rights.
The radically left-wing Students for a Democratic
Society (SDS) created large chapters on college
campuses and frequently took over buildings and
staged riots.

Rabbi Kahane and members of The JDL

Given this historical backdrop, it is not
surprising that Rabbi Kahane, *ztk'l* (of blessed
memory), keenly observed the tenor of the times
and the political zeitgeist that wafted in the air. He
knew that at this juncture in history, the time had
arrived for the Jew to champion his rights and to
immerse himself in causes that were imperative for
the survival of Jews around the globe. "JDL is a

movement whose time has come," said Rabbi Kahane in the summer of 1968 when he founded The JDL.

The success of The Jewish Defense League lies in the fact that Rabbi Kahane had his finger on the pulse of America's youth and knew that anti-war sentiments, civil rights movements, and other demonstrations were top-heavy with young Jews seeking a cause to fight for. He then said, "If the Jewish young person is looking for a cause to fight for, let's give him a Jewish cause to fight for."

The ever alert and vigilant Rabbi Meir Kahane

Jewish youth were tired of being given things such as JCC basketball leagues, parties, or events that ostensibly drew them to involvement in the Jewish community because such efforts proved to be an abysmal failure. Rather, Rabbi Kahane would often say that "for the Jewish youth, we are calling upon him and her to give to their own People, to sacrifice for their own People, to dedicate themselves to the interests of their own People." He added that "if the Jewish youth wants to get arrested for a cause, then join JDL, and we guarantee you a cause to get arrested for." Jewish youth flocked to The JDL to fight for Jewish causes because, at the end of the day, the true fulfillment of the Jewish soul is inextricably tied to giving to others and achieving things that were never thought possible.

In relation to this, Rabbi Kahane often told the story of a huge JDL demonstration in Washington, D.C. in

which hundreds of young Jews were arrested for
sitting in the streets in support of the liberation of
Soviet Jews. Rabbi Kahane was among the
arrested. In the jail cell with him was a large group
of Jewish youngsters and a young Jewish man with
long hair and no yarmulke who stood in a corner
of the cell by himself and cried. Rabbi Kahane
thought that he might be scared and so went to
him to console him, saying, "Look, there is
nothing to be afraid of. I have been through this
many times and before you know it, they will let us
out."

The young man replied, "Rabbi Kahane, I
am not crying because I am afraid of getting
arrested. I am crying because I am overcome with
emotion with the thought of what I have just
done: this is the first time in my life that I have
ever done anything to help my People."

Rabbi Kahane, members of The JDL, and the ever-present "Jewish Fist"

Above & Below: Rabbi Kahane speaking with passion and pride.

Right: The Rabbi on the streets of New York

93

Rabbi Kahane speaking to the press about the mission of The Jewish Defense League

Rabbi Kahane and members of The JDL take their message to the streets

Rabbi Kahane speaks about the mission of The JDL

Rabbi Kahane rallies members of The JDL

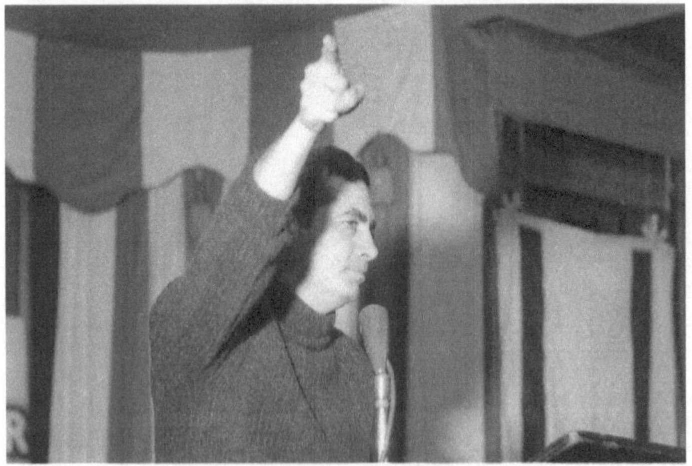

The Rabbi speaking passionately

Rabbi Kahane serving as teacher and mentor to members of The JDL.

26

KAHANE KORNER: MARTIAL ARTS AND THE JEWISH WARRIOR

"In the practice of Krav Maga, we don't ask 'What can be done?' - as that implies a sense of helplessness; we ask 'What will we do?' - because that carries with it the notion of a direct action we can take."

Moshe Katz, Master Krav Maga Instructor and Author

Upon its inception, The Jewish Defense League was envisaged by Rabbi Meir Kahane as a vehicle for teaching physical self-defense techniques to the Jewish People. Building on the paramilitary training model provided years before by Ze'ev Jabotinsky's **Camp Betar**, Rabbi Kahane and The Jewish Defense League steadfastly set about teaching martial arts to young Jews, establishing formal karate classes and training camps everywhere. Some of the youth camps provided up to four hours of karate training a day.

Today, many Jews train in a martial art known as **Krav Maga** (pronounced Krahv-Muh-GAH). Meaning "Contact Combat," Krav Maga was originally developed specifically for the Israeli Defense Forces and focuses on techniques for reality-based attack situations.

As a rule, physical confrontation should be avoided and violence used only when absolutely necessary in self-defense; when it is impossible to avoid, the Jewish Warrior uses techniques to fight as quickly and aggressively as possible in order to then leave the dangerous situation.

Irv Rubin, National Chairman of The Jewish Defense League, famously remarked, "Whether it's mace or martial arts or firearms – we believe it's better to know how and not have to, then to have to and not know how."

Members of The JDL engaging in self-defense exercises and techniques

Above: JDL members strength-trained together

Right: Members also practiced martial arts

JDL members preparing to begin a self-defense drill

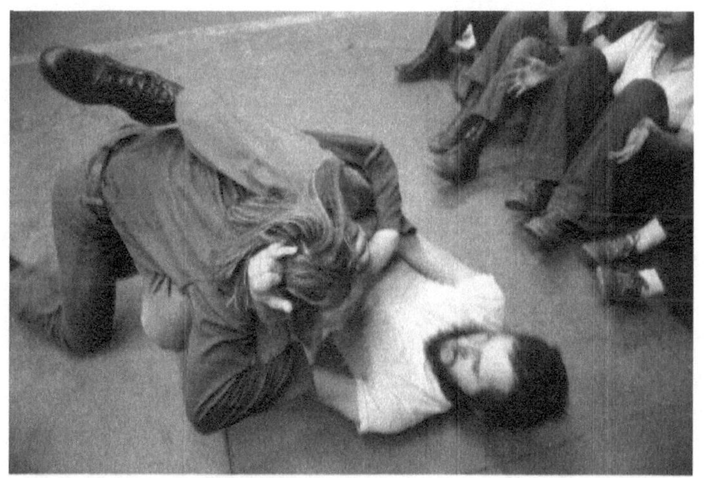

Members of The JDL grappling and learning how to fight

27

IRV RUBIN

"Irv never cowered in fear, he never retreated from his righteous position. He stood firm and stared his enemies in the face. Irv was a proud Jew, even when Nazi thugs threatened to turn him into a lampshade. That was Irv Rubin."

Fern Sidman, Jewish Defense League Leader

With the notable exception of JDL Founder Rabbi Meir Kahane, no one served as a more passionate voice or public face for The Jewish Defense League than Irv Rubin. Whether it was punching a neo-Nazi on live television or singlehandedly preventing a group of thugs from desecrating a Jewish cemetery with his baseball bat, Irv Rubin was there. He repeatedly placed himself in stark opposition to the anti-Semite to announce that the Jewish People would

Above: Irv Rubin, National Chairman of The Jewish Defense League

Above & subsequent photos courtesy of the Rubin Family

no longer go down without a fight.

Irv Rubin was a fearless man and a brave warrior devoted to the dignity and survival of his People. Let us further explore his life through the words and memories of his wife and fellow JDL leader Shelley Rubin.

Interview with Shelley Rubin, President of The Jewish Defense League Las Vegas, February 2015

ROSS BERG: Can you tell me how Irv Rubin got involved in The Jewish Defense League (JDL)?

SHELLEY RUBIN: The first time, to my knowledge, that Irv was involved in The Jewish Defense League was in 1970. He attended a lecture by JDL Founder Rabbi Meir Kahane at California State University, Northridge. And Irv said, "I had always felt what this man was talking about!" So, when Rabbi Kahane was finished with his speech that day, Irv stuck around. And when the two of them spoke, there was a connection right away. And Rabbi Kahane knew he had someone good. Kahane knew he had a wonderful guy right here! So at that moment, this bond between Irv and JDL formed and Irv got involved right away. There was already a Los Angeles JDL. There were other people who had followed Rabbi Kahane from the beginning. But Irv joined in 1970 and by '71 he was named West Coast Coordinator of The Jewish Defense League.

RB: How did you and Irv first meet?

SR: When I was in high school, I remember seeing Irv on local TV shows and if there were Nazis there, there would be fights. And I was really proud. I was proud that Jews

were finally standing up for themselves. From the time I
was a kid, the only thing important to my father was that I
marry a Jewish guy. So, when I got to high school –
Arcadia High School in Southern California – it was three
percent Jewish. And I said, "Well Dad, how do I date
somebody Jewish around here? There aren't any Jews."
And he said, "I don't know. Go to the synagogue." And
my mom said, "There must be a youth group there." And,
darn it, I did. So, I joined the B'nai B'rith Youth
Organization for girls, and I didn't know much about
Judaism. My family was very, very assimilated. Almost
embarrassingly so. And I always felt something was
missing. I remember having a discussion with the youth
coordinator about inviting JDL to come down. At the
same time, I was afraid because everyone said, "Don't get
involved in JDL because you won't be able to go to
college if you get arrested!" Around that time, my friend
and I used to go up to Los Feliz and Sunset. There was a
liquor store and Irv happened to be there and he was
wearing green military khaki. He was talking to somebody
on the phone and I said to him, "Are you Irv Rubin?"
And he just kind of looked at me and nodded with a
serious expression. And I said, "Oh, you do a great job."
This had to be in '74. Now, after college, I got a job as a
bookkeeper with a corporation in Century City and so I
was finally able to pay my rent myself. I lived in
Brentwood, California and my life was pretty good… I
mean, I didn't have any responsibilities. At that time, there
was friction brewing in the African-American community
with them backing Jesse Jackson, who had called Judaism
"a gutter religion." Jesse Jackson went and met with
Palestinian Leader Yasser Arafat and it started worrying
me. I said, "What organizations are addressing this issue?"
I only saw one. And it was JDL.

So, I met Irv… and I remember when I went to the office – the office was located on Fairfax upstairs above a nut shop. Anytime you were there, it smelled like nuts! I walked into the office and one of The JDL guys was there because I had made an appointment. He called Irv and said, "Get down here right away!" It was nice to be a female around all these guys. Irv was very persistent and I said, "I don't want to date you because, you know, it's not good." You see, when my parents said to me, "We want you to marry a nice Jewish boy," they really weren't figuring I would find an Irv Rubin type of guy. But he wore me down. Irv was such a nice guy… just such a nice, nice guy.

RB: So, was Irv Rubin known then? Would your parents have known who he was when you mentioned you were dating him?

SR: Oh yeah. Yes.

RB: What was Irv's background prior to joining The Jewish Defense League?

SR: Irv's parents named him Irving Seymour Rubin when he was born on April 12, 1945 in Montreal, Canada. That's the date that Franklin Delano Roosevelt (FDR) died. You will find no monuments to President Roosevelt in Israel because he could have done so much more for the Jews during the Holocaust and he didn't. He turned ships of Jews away back to their deaths. But who was born the same day as FDR? I was born on January 30 and that was FDR's birthdate. So that was really weird when Irv and I compared that. Irv's father Morris was from Canada and passed away a few years after Irv. He lived through my husband's death. Irv's mother was Doris. Doris Feldman.

It's so cute how they rhyme: Morris and Doris. She was from London and worked as a nurse in the Civil Defense Corps while the war was going on and Morris was in the Royal Canadian Air Force… That's how they met. They named their son Irving Seymour and as a kid, he certainly did experience anti-Semitism; having a name like Irving Seymour didn't help. When Irv was a kid, he remembered seeing a sign in a window that said, "No Jews or Dogs Allowed." And as a kid, from that moment on, he didn't feel comfortable anymore in Canada. Irv was six or seven years old when he came home crying and told his mother that there was a kid who called him a "Christ Killer" and hit him. And his mother Doris yelled at Irv, "Don't you ever let them get the better of you! You wash your face off, go back out there, and beat the crap out of him!" She sent Irv back out to find the kid. And he never lost a fight after that… 'til the very end.

Irv's mother and I butted heads over the years but I have to give credit where credit is due: his mother made him a fighter. When I was a kid, I cried all the time and I wish someone had taken me and said, "Stop crying! It's a sign of weakness. Don't do that!" It took me a long time. I can't cry anymore. Irv's family was a typical Jewish family. Real liberal politically. They had Shabbat every Friday night… They celebrated all the holidays… They were conservative Jews. Being Jewish was very important to his family.

Irv wasn't the best student. He said, "I couldn't tell you one thing about Canadian history. But I can name you all the amendments of the U.S. Constitution." He loved the U.S. When Irv was a kid, he dreamed of coming to America. He loved U.S. history. Irv and his family came to America when he was about 14. Irv said one of the happiest days of his life was when his family moved to the U.S. They settled into Northridge, California and he went to Granada Hills High School. He played on the football team and worked at a burger joint and was a regular normal kid. So, years later, while he was in the U.S. Air Force, Irv became a U.S. citizen; he got his citizenship by being in the Air Force. And when he did the paperwork to become a citizen, he took that opportunity to change his middle name Seymour to David. Irv became a sergeant in the Air Force and he worked in Repro… the Reproduction Department – copying and printing classified information – so he had to have high security clearance.

RB: We all know Irv the 'Street Fightin' Activist,' but what was your husband like when he was out of the spotlight?

SR: Oh, was-was… he was just a good man. An upright person. He was a very, very devoted husband and father. Loved us very much. He had no taste in music. All he listened to was fifties doo-wop stuff. He loved dogs – even when they destroyed our carpets. He loved coffee. He didn't like how I made coffee. I tried. I bought every coffee maker… I just couldn't. We had many good friends, friends who were and weren't Jewish.

Irv and Shelley Rubin on their wedding day, 1980

Irv wasn't a drinker but we went to a New Year's Eve
party and they convinced him to drink and he almost
knocked over the Christmas Tree. That was the first and
last time I ever saw him inebriated.

On our honeymoon, we decided to drive
up north and we stayed at the Madonna Inn. We're
having a wonderful time and we go up to Carmel
and to San Francisco and then Irv got a phone call.
It seems a couple of The JDL guys got arrested for
stealing a Torah from Jews For Jesus. So, we drove
back home to help The JDL folks out of their jam.
Anything for JDL. It was never a dull moment
with Irv Rubin! Irv was very driven. You know, he
didn't sleep very much. Denny's Restaurant is
open all the time and was close to where we lived,
so Irv would, like, "hold court" with his friends
and they would just talk excitedly about politics at
Denny's at 3 a.m. in the morning. He was always
kind to people; unless you were a Jew-hater, Irv
would be very respectful to you. My husband
would be walking down the street and if somebody
said, "Can you help me?" he would reach into his
pocket and give what he had. That's the kind of
person Irv was. And I think people took advantage
of that.

When Irv was home, he was the best
father, the best husband, the best everything. But
sometimes he wasn't home. He had to do things.
And I never told him he couldn't because that's
who I married. He just always had Jewish things
on his mind. The family did take a back seat, but
that was okay because that's who he was. And, of
course, it was more fun in the beginning when I
could go with him and do all The JDL activities
alongside him. And that's how we lived. By his

fundraising. Irv lived and breathed JDL. He was so
focused and committed. Before he would go on TV or
radio, you could see him mouth the words that he wanted
to say. Whenever he was a guest on a talk show, the
phones would just light up. When Irv didn't have the news
on 24/7, he was listening to talk radio. Sometimes he
would be compelled to call in and they would say, "Oh, we
have Irv Rubin on the line!" He was those talk show hosts'
dream.

RB: Did Irv have any contact with Holocaust survivors in
his family growing up? If so, did that motivate him to
ultimately get involved with JDL?

SR: Yes, it did. One of Irv's closest relatives was his Uncle
Max. Max Frajberg. He was a Holocaust survivor. Irv was
very, very close to that particular uncle. When Rabbi
Kahane ran JDL, the big place was New York. Kahane
was headquartered there. Everything came out of New
York. So, Irv would have to go to New York and when he
did, he would stay at Aunt Ann and Uncle Max's house.
And his Uncle Max would tell Irv what it was like in the
concentration camps. The horror of the concentration
camps. Irv got it first-person from a Holocaust survivor.

RB: Can you tell me about your experiences with Rabbi
Meir Kahane?

SR: I met Rabbi Kahane on many occasions. The first time
was before Irv and I got married; the Rabbi wanted to
meet me and talk with me. It was a bit intimidating
walking into this big room at the Crest Hotel and the
Rabbi was sitting in this chair with all these people around
waiting to talk to me. When Rabbi Kahane opened his
mouth, you knew you were in the presence of a bigger-

than-life person. You really did. He was a very, very nice person. He was funny. Very funny. He had kind eyes. But he was not perfect, either. He had a tic. He'd blink his eyes. He would jiggle the change in his pockets while he was speaking which drove me a little crazy. But people were in awe of him. You really were in awe when Rabbi Kahane was around. And I know there were people who were very much in awe when Irv Rubin was around… but when you're married to the person, you don't think of them as larger-than-life – they're just another person.

But Rabbi Kahane…he had kind eyes, but I think there was hurt there, too. Irv would have done anything for the Rabbi. They would talk on the phone and they spent a lot of time together when Rabbi Kahane was in Los Angeles to raise money. The two of them really believed in the cause 100 percent. Neither of them felt like anything was more important than the Jewish People.

RB: Did Irv follow the "Tenets of Kahane" or did he take The JDL in a different direction?

SR: Irv was always true to JDL ideology. *Ahavot Yisroel:* the love of one Jew for another. The principle that all Jews are part of the great body, Israel. The pain of a Jew, wherever he is, is our pain; the joy of a Jew, wherever he is, is our joy. Pride in, and knowledge of, Jewish tradition. The changing of the Jewish image from that of the weakling to one who refuses to be stepped on. Faith in the indestructibility of the Jewish people. The main issues for JDL were freedom for Soviet Jewry, support of Israel, the safety of the Jews, dealing with neo-Nazis and your Jew-hating neighbor who spray-paints a swastika on your property.

RB: Rabbi Kahane did many interviews in his lifetime and wrote a multitude of articles and books outlining his thoughts and beliefs. Irv Rubin is under-represented in this area. What were some of Irv's philosophies?

SR: Irv always liked to say that Jews should model themselves after those in the Israel Defense Forces because the bullies go after the weak. He didn't want Jews to be weak and terrorized. Irv also believed that when it came to JDL, you don't idolize the man; you have to be in it for the ideology. There were a lot of people who just loved to hang onto Rabbi Kahane and go see him speak and all that, but they didn't do anything else. We'd say, "You know, we're demonstrating for Israel" and they'd say, "No, we don't have time for that," but they'd be going nuts over Rabbi Kahane as a person. And Irv understood that, but he didn't feel that that was the right reason for being a part of JDL. Irv always said, "You don't follow the man, you follow the philosophy of what the man is saying." Otherwise, it's just a cult of personality; it becomes people wanting to hang around a celebrity without doing the hard work.

RB: What drove Irv to be so visible as JDL's leader?

SR: Well, you know, Irv did all of this before the internet. So, he needed to be on TV and the radio to spread JDL's message. And he made a lot of news wherever he went. But Irv's motivation wasn't to get his face on television or his name in the paper. There were lots of times when he laid low for the greater good. There was a guy named Richard Butler in Idaho who led a group of neo-Nazis up there and they were causing trouble. Irv was going to bring The JDL there to confront them, but Morris Dees, the head of The Southern Poverty Law Center, asked Irv to work with him and to not get involved so that he could get Butler shut down.

Irv cooperated with Dees, even though he could have gotten a lot of headlines for himself if that's all he wanted – but he realized that they had a better chance of stopping Butler if there was no publicity attached to the move beforehand. Morris Dees later wrote Irv a letter in appreciation. And there were many things that Irv got involved with that had nothing to do with Jews.

If you remember, there were these two college kids who went to Las Vegas and one of them killed a little girl in a casino bathroom and the other guy, his friend, knew about it but didn't turn in him. Well, Irv partnered with radio hosts Tim Conway Jr. and Doug Steckler to launch a petition campaign to demand that authorities file charges against that friend as an accessory to that seven-year-old girl's murder.

Author Ross Berg interviewing Shelley Rubin

RB: What made Irv Rubin so fearless?

SR: Nobody was too big or bad for Irv to be afraid of. I don't know where that comes from. You know, he just had guts. I think he called it "Intestinal Fortitude."

RB: Did you fear for your husband's safety on those television shows or during public demonstrations?

SR: I always felt that God would look after him.

RB: What do you say to critics of The JDL and especially Jewish ones?

SR: They have a right to feel any way they want. The problem is, they're making it very easy for enemies of the Jews to destroy us. And the big mainstream Jewish organizations that were publicly critical of us knew that they secretly needed JDL. I cannot tell you how many times Irv got calls in the middle of the night from the Anti-Defamation League (ADL) about stuff that the ADL was passing on to him to take care of. They knew they secretly needed JDL. All of them did.

RB: Why do you feel The JDL is so important?

SR: I know that JDL isn't for every person and that's okay, but we've always been motivated by our belief that we have to take care of each other. And that's the first principle of JDL. As Jews, we have to have each other's backs. People have to feel safe. I feel that there are always going to be Jews who choose not to live in Israel. I do think the best place for Jews to be is in Israel, but that's just not how it's going to be. And JDL was created by Rabbi Kahane as an organization for the Galut, for the Diaspora. Those in exile need protection. In Israel, they have JDL. It's called the Israel Defense Forces. So, Jews, elsewhere in the world, have to have an organization that they can call on, just in case. And that's why we always must support The JDL and enable people who are willing to stand up for other Jews.

People wake up too late. I don't see terrorism against Jews decreasing. What's to keep a terrorist from walking into a Jewish establishment with a suicide vest? They will. I really feel they will. I'm afraid they will. There are lots of threats to the Jewish people, but I have a faith in God that we'll survive one way or another. A lot of us have faith in the indestructibility of the Jewish People – that's one of our tenets. I have faith in God's protection but I also know that we, as Jews, must work to protect one another.

28

KAHANE KORNER: PASSING THE TORCH

"Let new Jewish Leaders arise."

Rabbi Meir Kahane, Founder of The Jewish Defense League

Focusing his energies toward a political career in Israel, Rabbi Kahane ultimately turned leadership responsibilities over to Irv Rubin, making Irv the new National Chairman of The JDL. Below is a copy and content of a letter from Kahane to Rubin.

January 3, 1974
9, Tenet 5734

Dear Irv,

Firstly, my deepest thank you for all the efforts of The JDL in Los Angeles. Life is hard but victory is always there in the end.

You are doing fine work and I hope that I will yet be able to see you in America.

Very best to all,

Meir Kahane

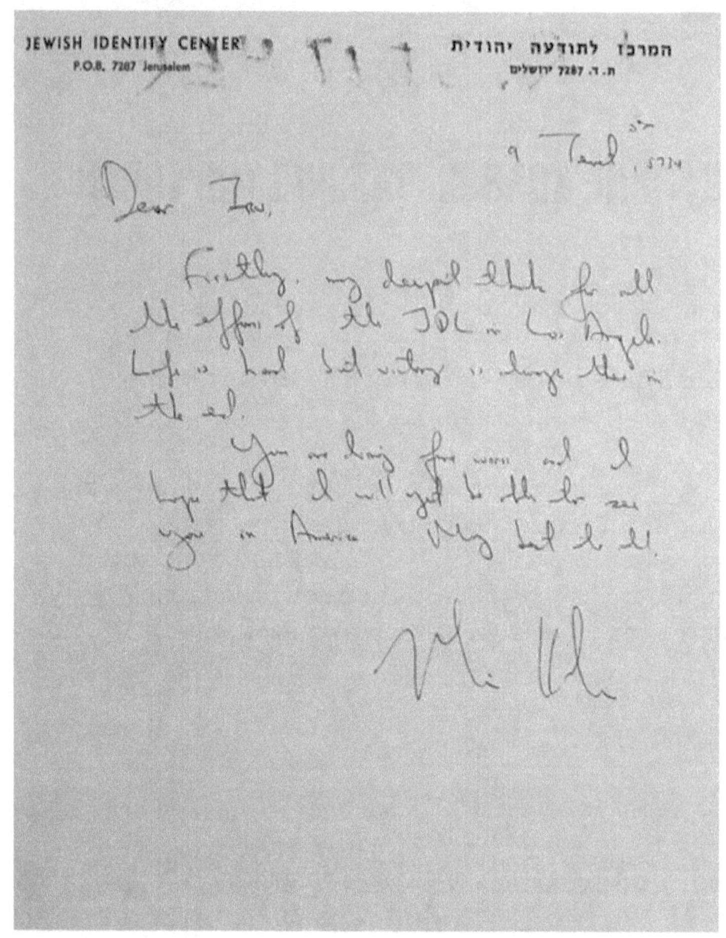

The letter Meir Kahane wrote to Irv Rubin, from the author's private collection

29

SKOKIE

"The only thing hateful people understand is to beat the living hell out of them. I felt it had to be met 'force with force'. And I watched and I noticed that some of the Nazis, after taking terrible beatings, didn't come back. It was painful to get beaten."

Buzz Alpert, Chairman: Chicago Jewish Defense League

In 1978, a group of Neo-Nazis decided to march in Skokie, Illinois. The location was specifically and strategically selected because it was the home of 7,000 survivors of the Holocaust, thus containing the largest percentage of survivors in any town within all of America. The goal of the Neo-Nazis was to make the Jewish survivors feel that even after the Holocaust was over and even after they had found a haven in America that they were still not safe and that they would never be safe.

During the early planning stages of the march, the Neo-Nazis showed up in full Nazi uniforms, waved the Swastika flag, and plastered the city with leaflets which read: "We're Coming to Get You," "Smash the Jew," and "Six Million More."

Seeking to intimidate and degrade the Holocaust survivors in the area to maximum effect, the Neo-Nazis selected Adolph Hitler's birthday to march, later changing the planned date to coincide with the Passover holiday. All of this was designed to frighten these survivors and make them feel that the nightmare of the Holocaust would never fade for them.

The intended march in Skokie marked the day that the sons and daughters of Holocaust survivors stood together and confronted a legacy of evil. Largely made up of survivors and their families, the members of The Jewish Defense League had grown up with parents who awoke screaming in the night from the terrors they had experienced. This was their time to confront the ghosts of their parents' past – to stand up for them and, in some cases, with them as they stared down those who sought to destroy them once and for all.

Prior to the official march, the Neo-Nazis came to the little town to better scope out the surroundings and logistics. The Jewish Defense League showed up in force. Local leaders advised the Jewish community to simply go to their homes, draw the blinds, and ignore the situation, pointing out that there were really only a small number of Nazis in attendance anyway. But these survivors had heard that speech before when they had been persuaded to not make waves over just "a small number of Nazis" prior to the Holocaust. Never Again.

Speaking to the assembled crowd, Rabbi Meir Kahane said, "We spit on the graves of six million Jews if we allow the Nazis to march." JDL Leader Irv Rubin arrived with a large group of members from Los Angeles and – led by **Buzz Alpert**, the head of Chicago JDL – the Nazis experienced the power of the Jewish fist that afternoon. Battered and bleeding, the Nazis fled the town of Skokie.

Although vowing to return, the Neo-Nazis never did march in Skokie, Illinois. Some historical accounts credit the court system for thwarting the

Nazis' efforts by complicating and delaying their ability to secure the proper permits. But, in the end, the Neo-Nazis utterly feared for their lives based on the involvement of The Jewish Defense League and begged Illinois leaders to find them an alternate site.

The Neo-Nazi march in Skokie, Illinois was designed to be a cruel reminder to a town of Holocaust survivors that they could run, but they could not hide — that they would never be free from their cycle of torment; that they would never be free from Nazi victimhood; and that the Holocaust and its potential to return would never be over for them.

What the Nazis did not count on was the way in which their effort of evil actually galvanized the Jewish community. Not only did Jews come together in an incredible display of force to chase their enemies out of town, but the entire incident led to a renewed awareness and discussion of the Holocaust in America.

Major television movies and mini-series on the topic began to be broadcast as Holocaust memorials and museums were constructed in an effort to spread awareness. Schools made it mandatory that all students learn about one of humanity's greatest tragedies to ensure that such evil would never be repeated.

Self-defense patrols of The JDL.

Rabbi Kahane speaks to the press about the mission of The JDL

Members of The JDL, including Meir Kahane, take to the streets

Members gather as Rabbi Kahane rallies the group

Above: Rabbi Kahane on the loud speaker

Right: Kahane with the "Jewish Fist," "Never Again!"

Above: Well-known Kahane rejoices at the gathering of JDL members

Right: The Rabbi addressing the crowd

30

KAHANE KORNER: THE PERILS OF SILENCE AND RESPECTABILITY

"The world is a dangerous place, not because of those who do evil, but because of those who look on and do nothing."

Albert Einstein, Jewish Nobel Prize-Winning Physicist

Rabbi Meir Kahane urged Jews everywhere to expose and speak out loudly against anti-Semitism wherever it festered, no matter how large or small the group spreading the hate. The great Rabbi continuously cautioned fellow activists of the foolishness and danger in assuming that if a hate group is small, it should be ignored; after all, the Hitler era began with just 12 people.

"Never Again." Rabbi Kahane's famous slogan meant that if anyone tried to repeat the Holocaust, never again would it be met with the same fear or lack of reaction. Never again would the Jewish community sit silently by, for silence in the face of evil is always a guarantee of disaster and misery for the victims in question.

For too long, Jews, being strangers in strange lands, concerned themselves with blending in with polite society and in not making waves. The goal was to be seen as respectable, but respectability kills when it leads to passivity in the face of injustice.

In order to call attention to injustice, we must not be afraid of enduring the scorn of polite society. We must not be afraid to assemble, to raise our voices, to create a scene if necessary. Prior to the activism of The Jewish Defense League, modern politicians assumed Jews would passively accept their fate, not protest too strongly, and would certainly not become physical.

Under Rabbi Kahane's leadership, The JDL proved these assumptions and expectations false and forced the world to view the "passive Jew" in a new light. Angry and even violent demonstrations serve to arouse an ignorant or indifferent society to the dangers of impending evil and the anomaly of the modern Jew taking to the streets and causing an uproar was just the thing to get the media interested; thus, the media used the

Kahane and members of The JDL taking to the streets

exploits of The JDL to sell newspapers and garner television ratings. Likewise, The JDL used the media to promote their agenda on page one of every media outlet around the world.

Never again would we be silent.

Never again would we allow an indifferent world to conveniently turn away.

In the words of Nobel Peace Prize-winning Holocaust survivor **Elie Wiesel**, "We must always take sides. Neutrality helps the oppressor, never the victim. Silence encourages the tormentor, never the tormented."

Rabbi Kahane, ever-impassioned

31

ISRAEL DEFENSE FORCES

"The Jews were thrown to the wind. Exterminated in Europe, expelled from Arabia. This vibrant democracy called Israel, sitting amidst a sea of failed states, how it sticks in the throat of the anti-Semite. After all they endured, how dare the Jews succeed!"

David Collier, Political Scientist

Just two weeks after Israel's rebirth and Declaration of Independence on May 31, 1948, the Israel Defense Forces (IDF) was established. From its inception, the IDF's primary purpose has been to defend Israel from the many hostile surrounding neighbors which vastly outnumber them. Due to its small size (Israel is roughly the size of the tiny state of New Jersey and is surrounded by 22 Muslim states that are 700 times the size of Israel!), Israel knows it cannot afford to lose even a single war. Yet on June 5, 1967, it looked as though such a scenario was going to play out.

Known today as **"The Six Day War,"** Israel came under the attack of five Arab armies... and won. This brief war was, by all accounts, a contemporary miracle. As it took the Lord six days to create the world, it took Israel the same length of time to defeat an enemy desperate to finish what Hitler had started; for it was not the land that the Arabs wanted so much as Jewish lives. Of the Six-Day War, Rabbi Kahane said, "Had we lost the war, the eulogies over Israel would have been among the most beautiful of all time. If you want sympathy, that's the way to do it. This time we figured, let's live. So we fought and we won and they condemn us for it. We prefer it that way. No more *Kaddish*. No more sympathy. *Let's live!*"

Harkening to Biblical times when Abraham assembled a small army and led it into battle against the armies of four kings, the brave members of the Israel Defense Forces similarly laid their lives on the line in order to preserve their sacred traditions and God-given land.

Still, there were more miraculous moments to come. In October 1973, Egypt and Syria used their combined forces to surprise-attack Israel on Yom Kippur, the holiest day of the Jewish calendar. Caught off-guard, the IDF was stunned to see the enemy rapidly crossing the Suez Canal with purpose and ferocity. With God on their side and the Warrior blood of the Maccabees flowing through the veins of the men and women of the IDF, Israel succeeded in disabling the enemies' air defenses and surrounding their giant army by water. As the Israel Defense Forces began transporting tanks across the Suez Canal on a floating bridge, the enemy admitted defeat to the small but mighty Land of Israel.

Three years later in 1976, two Germans belonging to an anti-Israel group hijacked an airplane traveling from Tel Aviv to Paris. After landing at the Entebbe Airport in Uganda, the hijackers released all of the non-Israelis but demanded $5 million for the release of the Israeli hostages. The Israel Defense Forces responded with a military plan called **Operation Entebbe**.

Led by **Yonatan Netanyahu**, the brother of future Israeli Prime Minister Benjamin Netanyahu, four

Hercules transporters accompanied by two jets were secretly flown to Uganda. The IDF arrived in Entebbe in the dead of night and released from the Hercules transporter vehicles adorned with Ugandan flags containing Israeli commandos in Ugandan uniforms.

Israeli soldiers began firing on the enemy with silenced pistols; unfortunately, one soldier using an unsilenced weapon inadvertently alerted the enemy to what was occurring and a brief gun battle took place. The hijackers were killed as were 20 Ugandan soldiers. Sadly, the heroic Yonatan Netanyahu also lost his life that day. Considered a stunning success, all 102 Israeli hostages boarded a plane to return to their Jewish homeland. What the IDF accomplished that day in 1976 is still taught and studied by armies around the globe. Operation Entebbe would later be renamed **Operation Yonatan** in honor of the great Warrior and head commander Yonatan Netanyahu.

From destroying Iraq's nuclear arsenal in the 1980s to saving 14,500 Ethiopian Jews in the 1990s via **Operation Solomon** to today's miraculous rocket interceptions, the IDF continues to be one of the mightiest and most formidable military entities on Earth. Its Warriors, both men and women, can mobilize quickly due to the compact size of the country and its Air Force has been ranked first in the entire world. Israel's **Iron Dome Defense System** intercepts rockets regularly from its hostile neighbors, protecting Jewish lives in highly populated areas.

Working in close collaboration with the IDF is the **Mossad** (pronounced Moe-Sod), Israeli Intelligence, Counter-Terrorism, and elite trained covert operatives devoted to the protection and survival of the People of Israel.

Military analysts and historians continue to be amazed by the IDF's many successes, but it is clear that the Jewish People have A Friend in High Places.

Israel is a shining beacon of freedom and the only democracy in the entirety of the Middle East. God gave us the Land of Israel. And we will forever cherish it and protect it.

32

MODERN-DAY JEWISH DEFENSE LEAGUE: INTERNATIONAL

"The Jewish Defense League was born out of necessity to protect our Community. When it came time to protect fellow Jews in need, The JDL acted without hesitation; and that instantly defined the heroism of the Organization."

Aharon Hadida, JDL Canada

In 1977, a 20-year-old Canadian named **Meir Halevi Weinstein** read a book called *Never Again!* which changed his life. Written by JDL Founder Rabbi Kahane, this book mapped the history of Jewish oppression and the need to fight back against future oppression in electrifying fashion.

Accepting Rabbi Kahane's written call to take a stand and get involved, young Meir Halevi Weinstein started The Conference of Jewish Activists in Toronto. Three years later, Weinstein went to Yeshivah in Israel to learn directly from the great Rabbi, furthering his understanding and commitment to the indestructibility of the Jewish People, the need for Jewish unity, the importance of self-defense, the love of Israel, and the unique pride and dignity connected to being a Jew.

In 1981, Rabbi Kahane spoke to a packed crowd of synagogue members and curious guests at Shaarei Tefillah Synagogue in Toronto, Canada; there, he passionately articulated the dangers of assimilation, the need for stronger Jewish education, and the critical importance of every Jew ultimately returning to live in Israel. Amongst the packed crowd was Meir Halevi Weinstein who, by then, had decided to devote his life to the tenets of The Jewish Defense League. He became the National Director of JDL Canada in 1979.

Under the focused leadership of Weinstein, JDL Canada began to identify and bring to justice Nazi war criminals living and hiding out in Canada. They also set about providing free security and protection for elderly Jews and local synagogues, especially during the High Holy Days.

JDL Canada remains extremely active under Weinstein's leadership, successfully counter-protesting and shutting down a myriad of anti-Semitic events. The branch reaches out to and counsels Jewish at-risk youth and teaches self-defense techniques to young Jews who are being targeted and bullied. Meir Halevi Weinstein uses social media effectively to keep followers apprised of both anti-Semitic threats and ways in which the community can come together to fight for Jewish rights and survival.

Tom Messchendorp of JDL Holland

Chapters of The Jewish Defense League continue to carry forward the legacy of Rabbi Meir Kahane the world over. In addition to the U.S. and

Canada, The JDL thrives in Germany, Sweden,
France, Denmark, Hungary, South Africa, and
Holland. **Tom Messchendorp** of JDL Holland
has said, "There is no special occasion necessary to
show we won't forget, won't forgive, and will fight
until the last man standing. I would gladly sacrifice
my life to save only one Jew who would ultimately
be able to tell the story of our People."

*Today's warriors of
The Jewish Defense
League Canada -
inspired by their
fearless leader Meir
Halevi Weinstein.*

*Photos of JDL
Canada courtesy of
Meir Halevi
Weinstein and JDL
Canada.*

JDL Leader Aharon Hadida

*Today's warriors of
The JDL*

33

KAHANE KORNER: A "SUPERMENSCH" FOR THE NEXT GENERATION

"By the mid-1930s there were increasingly growing numbers of comic book publishers. The undisputed kings of the genre were a few superheroes who fought to rid the world of evil. Behind them stood mainly Jewish immigrants - not only the publishers but also the creative artists, the writers and illustrators. They were responsible for the fact that Jewish content seeped - consciously or otherwise - into the characters, plots and illustrated worlds on display."

Nirit Anderman, Haaretz

As Jews, we are related to a multitude of real-life superheroes dating back to the time of the Holy Bible; we are of one blood with men and women who put the imaginary exploits of comic book characters to shame with their actual heroics and daring.

Interestingly, most of the greatest comic book superheroes were created by Jews; Jerome Siegel and Joseph Shuster, Jack Kirby, Bob Kane, Bill Finger, Charlie Gaines, and Stan Lee all devoted their careers to teaching young people the virtues of being a hero.

In 2010, Yeshiva of the Jewish Idea, based in Jerusalem, published a 50-page graphic novel

Miracle Man, from the author's private collection

Special thanks to "Yeshiva of the Jewish Idea"

called *Miracle Man* designed to educate children about the life and ideology of Rabbi Meir Kahane. In the tradition of our distinctly Jewish comic book heritage, *Miracle Man* is a remarkably effective teaching tool in the spirit of *The Book of Genesis* by R. Crumb and *Maus* by Art Spiegelman. *Miracle Man* allows the teachings of Rabbi Meir Kahane to come alive for a new generation of young people using colorful artwork, compelling lessons, and intriguing action. For Rabbi Kahane's teachings to reach the next generation through such a medium is truly a blessing.

34

ZIONIST MOTORCYCLE CLUBS

"One can't be Jewish without Israel."

Elie Wiesel, Author, Nobel Peace Prize Winner, Holocaust Survivor

Zionism is the belief in a Jewish State.

Anti-Zionism is the belief that the only People in the entire world who cannot have their own State are the Jewish People.

As such, anti-Zionism *is* anti-Semitism.

Remember, God is a Zionist; He chose a Land and a People at an exact instant in time, making Judaism and Israel one and the same and thus inseparable.

Some of the proudest Zionists in the world, as you might imagine, live in the Land of Zion – the Hebrew word for Israel. Many of these proud Zionists are colorful, brave military heroes who elect to travel in packs and live to kick up ancient dust.

Together they roam.

Clusters of leather-clad bikers on choppers and Harleys dotting the beautiful hills and valleys of Israel.

Patches depict the fierce image of the mighty Samson and drape rippling biceps as the sunlight glistens off of freshly inked tattoos of the eternal six-cornered Shield of David.

The Zionist Motorcycle Clubs of the Holy Land are comprised of graduates of elite units of the Israel Defense Forces, Navy Seals, Paratroopers, Special Anti-terror Units, and Police Forces. Together, they work to provide protection and security to Synagogues and to the Jewish community at large.

Bonded by their love of Judaism, these bands of motorcycle-riding brothers celebrate and relish the freedom of the only democratic country in the entirety of the Middle East whilst observing the sacred holidays and organizing the study of Torah.

All of these Zionist Motorcycle Clubs are made up of proud, strong, joy-filled, family-oriented Jews who have devoted their lives to serving their country militarily and to protecting their People by fighting crime and averting terrorism.

These are Jews who love the Land of Israel, protect their fellow countrymen, radiate Jewish strength, and pass on the laws of Torah to their children. They are heroes. They are Warriors. They are Zionists.

And their engines roar as a collective Lion of Judah throughout the Land that God commanded our People to possess.

Samson Riders, Tel-Aviv Chapter

This photo and subsequent photos within the chapter are courtesy of the Samson Riders Motorcycle Club

Samson Riders of Tel-Aviv

SAMSON RIDERS
MC
TEL-AVIV

35

FERN SIDMAN: ON BETAR, THE JEWISH DEFENSE LEAGUE AND THE IMPORTANCE OF JEWISH STRENGTH

"We needed a legion of people to answer the anti-Semite in the only language he understands."

Fern Sidman, Jewish Defense League Leader

Fern Sidman is a Journalist and Jewish Warrior whose history includes active membership in the Betar Youth Movement and in The Jewish Defense League.

Fern Sidman Interview
New York, June 2019

ROSS BERG: Why do you feel that an awareness of past and present Jewish heroes and Warriors is especially important for the next generation of young Jews to learn about?

FERN SIDMAN: There is no doubt in my mind that those who ignore the lessons of history are condemned to relive them. All of us stand on the shoulders of our courageous antecedents; if not for our Jewish heroes both past and present, we would have no one to guide us on the often-turbulent trajectory of activism and we would have no one to imbibe wisdom from or to inspire us to greater heights.

First and foremost, it should be duly noted that our greatest Jewish heroes lived on the pages of our Torah. It is only in Torah that we get a real grasp of Jewish leaders, with Jewish values guiding their every moment. We study Torah so that we can learn how a Jew behaves under any and all circumstances. We learn values such as honesty, loyalty, and decency from people who had accepted the yoke of Heaven upon themselves.

We learn the difference between Noah and Abraham our forefather; the Torah tells us that Noah walked with G-d[1] but Abraham walked in front of G-d. What does this mean? Noah was indeed righteous in his generation that was replete with sinners but he needed G-d to walk with him and guide him, lest he fall. In the case of Abraham, from the time he was a young child, he knew there was a G-d who created the world and all that is in it. Coming from a family of idolators, he became a dissident of sorts, opposing the belief in idolatry and paying the price for it. Despite this, he was able to walk in front of G-d; his faith was beyond powerful and indeed unwavering.

Besides Abraham, we know that our other patriarchs and matriarchs were courageous leaders who taught us of faith and commitment to our People.

In the Book of Shmuel in the prophets, we learn of the son of Jesse, the shepherd boy David. When he visited his brothers who were fighting the Plishtim in the

---

[1] Fern Sidman is a practicing Orthodox Jew. As a sign of reverence, it is customary for Orthodox Jews to write God as G-d. In respect of Fern Sidman's interview, all references to God throughout this chapter have been written in observance of this custom.

army of Saul, he came upon Goliath of Gath.
What was David's response? It was that of a true
Jewish leader who does not cower in fear. He said,
"Who is this uncircumcised Philistine who dares
taunt the army of the living G-d?" He then picked
up his slingshot and killed the giant in front of the
entire army.

Our majestic but often blood-stained
history is filled with Jewish leaders whose faith in
G-d galvanized them to take bold actions for their
People and for that, and much more, we are
grateful.

For our young people, especially in our
generation, when the temptations of life swirl
around them constantly, it is imperative that they
become familiar with our leaders, and to learn our
history and to connect in a very personal way with
their glorious heritage. The Torah tells us that
when we teach Torah we should "say it into the
ears of our children and their children." What does
this mean? This means that when we tell the
teachings of the Torah, it has to be personal and
intimate. When the person who is learning it feels
close to the teachings because of how they are
taught, then he or she will always gravitate toward
it as it is a personal experience.

RB: What do you say to Jewish critics of The Jewish
Defense League who are under the impression that we
should never answer our enemies with strength and that a
physical response of any kind is un-Jewish?

FS: The truth is that the goal of the Jew is to strive for
peace. Each day, we pray three times a day and at the end
of the *shemonei esrei*, we bow and take three steps back and

say the words, "*Oseh shalom bimromav, hu Yaaseh shalom aleinu v'al Kol Yisroel v'imru Amen.*"

This means that "you, G-d who made peace in the Heavens, please make peace here on earth." The word for heaven is *Shamayim*. It is a conjunction of two words, *Aish* (fire) and *Mayim* (water). G-d took two conflicting elements that normally cancel each other out and, through His infinite wisdom, created them to harmonize and work together. So too, here on earth, we have so many conflicting nations, so many major differences between us that we believe that we cannot co-exist. We beg G-d to allow us to make peace between us all. And this is why we take three steps back at this part of our prayers. For the sake of true peace, one cannot remain rigid and refuse to move. Those three steps back represent the fact that in order to achieve peace, we must compromise. We must not remain stubborn.

Having said that, we strive each day to establish peace between Israel and the nations of the world, despite the fact that we have so many differences.

G-d, in His infinite wisdom, also understood that the nations of the world have a blind and seething hatred toward us because we witnessed G-d and received the Torah at Sinai and they did not, even though they were given the opportunity to do so.

As a result, we the Jewish People have been targeted from time immemorial by those haters who seek our destruction. The timeless and eternal wisdom of the Torah gives us instruction on how to deal with our enemies. When Jacob met up with his brother Esau, who wanted to kill him, he prepared with three things: prayer, gifts, and he readied for war. If our attempts at making peace through diplomacy do not succeed, then we are obligated to defend ourselves with whatever means at our disposal and that includes physical strength and even in some circumstances, violence.

As Rabbi Kahane, *ztk'l* (of blessed memory), would often say, "Violence is a terrible thing but sometimes a terribly necessary thing." He also said that "violence is like money. It is not good or bad; it depends on how it is used."

This is why the Talmud says, "If someone comes to slay you, rise up and slay him first." Similarly, the Book of Vayikra directs, "Thou shall not stand idly by your brother's blood." If we see someone attempting to slay a Jew, we are obligated to defend him and kill his attacker.

This is why it tells us in the Book of Exodus that when Moses saw an Egyptian smiting a Jew, the verse says, "And Moses smote the Egyptian." As Rabbi Kahane often said, "That is a Jewish response to being attacked. Moses did not create a committee to study the root causes of anti-Semitism but rather he took it upon himself to save a Jewish life."

This is why the Hasmonean Dynasty and the Maccabees rose up and physically battled the Hellenized Assyrian-Greeks 200 years before the destruction of the Second Temple, as we read about in the story of Chanukah.

This is why we sing the beautiful song *Maoz Tzur* after lighting the Chanukah candles each night; this song praises the violence that we took against the Assyrian Greeks and praises our efforts to keep our faith alive.

When a Jew is attacked, humiliated, berated, and threatened with death and we do not do anything about it, then it is a *Chillul HaShem* (a desecration of G-d's name). The word *Chillul*

comes from the word *Challal*, which means "empty."
When we allow a Jew – including ourselves – to be
attacked and we do not fight back, then we have emptied
G-d from the world. In order to create a *Kiddush HaShem*
(to sanctify G-d's name) we must defend ourselves; we
must fight back; we must rise up with anger and righteous
indignation and defend ourselves.

So, in answer to your question, yes, the anti-Semite
in many cases, only understands physical strength, as
seeking agreement with him is at times impossible. And to
those Jewish critics and those purported Jewish leaders
who erroneously claim that there are no Jewish sources for
using physical strength to confront our enemies who seek
to vanquish us, then I say that these people are truly
ignorant of what a real Jewish concept is. Their narrow-
minded condemnations of Jews fighting back have led to
our destruction on many occasions. That is the painful
tragedy.

RB: Can you tell me a little bit about your experiences and
activities with Betar? How old were you and the other
participants, what did you learn, how did it change your
perceptions of your People and your history, and so forth?

FS: I joined the Brit Trumpeldor of America (Betar)
Zionist youth movement in the summer of 1971 when I
was 11 years old. I attended the annual eight-week summer
camp that the movement sponsored because my parents,
who were not affiliated with any Jewish political causes or
even a particular synagogue, wanted me to have exposure
to Jewish culture and to spend the summer with other
Jewish kids.

To this day, I truly believe that it was G-d who
guided me to Betar and I will tell you why. As I
mentioned, my parents were not Zionists, knew little

about Israel, and really had no politically
ideological beliefs; they decided that they would
ask the Jewish Federation to send them brochures
and information about all the Jewish camps in the
New York area.

Anyway, I recall that each day various
brochures arrived in the mail and they allowed me
to go through each one. After mulling through
them all, for some reason I chose Camp Betar,
even though I had no knowledge of the Betar
movement, of Ze'ev Jabotinsky, or Zionism for
that matter. The brochure just offered a basic
description of a camp like any other with
activities like arts and crafts, volleyball,
swimming, hiking, et cetera. Of course, they also
offered Israeli dancing, Hebrew lessons, and
synagogue services, and so forth. But

Jewish Defense League Leader Fern Sidman
Photo courtesy of Fern Sidman

then again, the other camps also offered these
activities as well but somehow, I chose Camp
Betar.

Little did I know it back then at the tender
age of 11, but this experience would define the rest
of my life in terms of commitment to my People,
the Land of Israel, and my dedication to Jewish
activism. It was at Camp Betar that I learned what
it meant to be a Jew, what was expected of me to

be a part of the glorious and majestic legacy of G-d's
treasured nation. I learned about the history of Zionism,
the Holocaust, the centuries-old scourge of anti-Semitism.
I learned of the formation of the modern State of Israel, as
well of Rosh Betar, Ze'ev Jabotinsky, of the heroism of
Joseph Trumpeldor. And I was educated about the
courageous Jews of the **Irgun** and the **Lechi**, also known
as **The Stern Gang**.

And most of all, I learned how imperative it was to
stand up for our People, to see myself as part of the family
of *Klall Yisroel* (all of Israel) and to sacrifice for them. In
the early-1970s, we all lived in the shadow of the
Holocaust and I was to meet many kids my age who were
children of Holocaust survivors.

The message was resoundingly clear: if the Jew
would not stand up and fight back against our enemies,
then no one else would. Just as the world totally
abandoned the Jew during the Holocaust years, so too
were we mandated to ensure that we would never be
passive in the face of Jew-hatred again. Many of us were
convinced that "it" could happen again as we imbibed the
stories from survivors of the unspeakable atrocities that
were wrought upon us by the Nazis.

After attending the camp, I began to join the
weekly Betar meetings in Brooklyn where I lived and
eventually began participating in demonstrations for the
freedom of Soviet Jews and all oppressed Jews, in defense
of Israel, and against anti-Semitic movements.

The very first demonstration I attended was
outside of the United Nations in September of 1972, after
the murder of 11 Israeli athletes at the Munich Olympic
Games by members of the terrorist Black September
Organization.

I also remember cutting school one day back in
February of 1976 to participate in a Betar takeover of the

Tass Office in New York City. Tass was the Soviet news agency. We took over their offices to protest the continued imprisonment of Soviet Jewish dissident **Doctor Mikhail Shtern**. Doctor Shtern had been sentenced to eight years of hard labor in Kharkiv after both his sons applied for visas to leave the Soviet Union for Israel.

Many demonstrations came after that and I ended up attending Camp Betar for eight years. I grew in its leadership ranks and served as a Division Head at the camp and eventually as Educational Director.

It was in Betar that I discovered a sense of self, of being part of a cause much larger than myself, and learning the requisite discipline to sacrifice of myself for others.

To this day, I still have my original Betar uniform hanging in my closet. I remain eternally indebted to the wonderful people in Betar who taught me that our purpose in life is to cleave to our people, our homeland, and our G-d.

When I was 18, I represented Betar at the American Zionist Youth Foundation's Machon L'Madrichei program in Jerusalem which consisted of a year of learning and living on a *moshav* (an Israeli agricultural community).

RB: Can you tell me about your first awareness of, and reactions to, The Jewish Defense League (JDL)?

FS: As a kid growing up in Brooklyn, I had heard of The JDL at about age eight or nine as I would see coverage of their demonstrations on the TV news. At that age, I really didn't know what to think and I certainly did not form an opinion as Jewish activism was not yet something that resonated with me. When I joined Betar a few years later, I began to understand the issues of the day that impacted the Jewish People and their survival, namely, anti-Semitism, strengthening Jewish identity when the forces of assimilation had claimed so many Jewish souls, the plight of oppressed Jews in the Soviet Union, Iraq, and Ethiopia, and the constant siege that Israel found herself under.

In the early-1970s when I was coming up in the world, we lived in the shadow of the Holocaust. The collective pain of our antecedents still haunted us and we knew it could all happen again.

RB: What were some of your first experiences of involvement with The Jewish Defense League?

FS: My first involvement with JDL was back in the late-1970s. I had met Rabbi Kahane while I was in Israel. I had attended a year-long program called Machon L'Madreichei that was sponsored by the American Zionist Youth Foundation and the educational program was geared toward leaders of Zionist youth groups. When I returned to the U.S., I began to attend JDL demonstrations and would often volunteer at The JDL office.

I recall that my first demonstrations were those that The JDL held outside of the Soviet Consulate on East 67th Street and Third Ave in Manhattan. We called for the freedom of such notable Jewish dissidents as **Yosef Begun, Sylva Zalmanson,** and **Anatoly Scharansky,** among others. I distinctly recall how the Soviets would film us from the rooftop of the building and how we would chant from the balcony of the Park East Synagogue which was located directly across the street. I also recall many demonstrations outside of the Israeli Consulate on 42nd Street and Second Ave. After the Nazis marched in Skokie, Illinois in 1977, I recall that we held a sit-in at the

ACLU offices in New York City as they were
providing a legal defense of the Nazis and their
right to call for the continued destruction of the
Jewish people.

RB: What were your personal impressions of Rabbi Meir
Kahane?

FS: I met Rabbi Kahane in 1978 and we maintained a
friendship until he was murdered in 1990. My impressions
of him was that he was a brilliant man, a true *talmid chocham*
(a student of sages) and *yiras shamayim* (awe of heaven). He
was a natural-born leader, a man gifted by G-d with a
palpable charisma, an ability to address audiences and
move people to action. His keenly astute analyses of the
times and of Jewish issues was beyond remarkable in so
many ways. He was a very friendly, kind, and generous
man, a man of great compassion, wisdom and prescience
(the fact of knowing something before it takes place) and
definitely a man who was lightyears ahead of his time.

RB: Did you ever have an official title or position with
The Jewish Defense League? If so, can you provide details
of your duties and experiences?

FS: In June of 1983, Rabbi Kahane and the board of
directors of JDL appointed me as National Director of
JDL. My predecessor, **Meir Jolovitz**, was leaving his post
to make *aliya* (immigration into Israel) with his family. I
remained in that position until September of 1985. We ran
the organization out of an office on Kings Highway in
Brooklyn. It was there that we held weekly classes in JDL
ideology, Jewish history, of the weekly Torah portion,
Halacha (the laws of Jewish life), as well as classes in the
martial arts and weight lifting, among other things.

It was within these four walls that strategy was planned, board meetings were held, and young people not only received an education on Jewish identity, but lifelong friendships were formed.

During the two-plus years that I was National Director of The JDL, the issues we focused on were many, but the main ones were the freedom of Soviet Jewry; seeking justice for Holocaust survivors by demanding that the Justice Department deport Nazi war criminals; organizing patrols around Yeshiva University where anti-Semitism had reared its ugly head as well as in Hartford, Connecticut and other areas; battling missionaries who were seeking to convert newly arrived Russian Jews; and initiating our nationwide campaign to expose the seething Jew-hatred of particular politicians.

RB: Libby Kahane has written some incredibly important and illuminating books about her husband Rabbi Kahane and The Jewish Defense League and you are acknowledged in these books. Can you give us any insights into your experiences with the Rebbetzin and in aiding her in the research or writings of these books?

FS: A number of years ago, I received an e-mail from Rebbetzin Kahane asking me questions about my remembrances of certain Jewish Defense League events, demonstrations and speaking dates of Rabbi Kahane. I believe that she had also asked me about some people who are involved in JDL and about Rabbi Kahane's books.

In a very long series of frequent and detailed e-mail correspondences that lasted for well over a year between myself and Rebbetzin Kahane, I provided answers to her questions and even did my own research on JDL events that I could not recall with total clarity. As soon as I would supply the answers to her questions, she would ask even more questions and I would answer those questions and give her sources as well. And this cycle repeated itself over and over again. I was more than pleased and very honored to play a role in this noble endeavor and actually enjoyed helping her very much.

At times, she would ask me what I recalled personally and if I could put her in touch with others who may have knowledge of events that she needed more information on.

I will say that her research was beyond impeccable in just about every way. The books she produced about Rabbi Kahane, after years of nuanced and painstaking research, were highly impressive scholarly monographs that have taken their place in the corpus of well received biographies of Jewish leaders.

RB: Rabbi Meir Kahane is incredibly important and his legacy speaks for itself, but I also want our young people to know about the vital work of another great leader within The Jewish Defense League: Irv Rubin. Can you tell me about your working relationship, friendship, and general impressions of Irv Rubin?

FS: I first met Irv Rubin, of blessed memory, the chairman of the Los Angeles chapter of The JDL back in the late-1970s when he visited the New York chapter of The JDL. Irv's legacy preceded him. He was known throughout the country as an intrepid spokesman and exceptionally dedicated activist for his People.

Irv employed a vast array of highly innovative and creative methods in organizing demonstrations that would capture the attention of the media; you might say that he excelled in political street theater. Irv was a constant figure on the news in LA, as he boldly and unflinchingly confronted anti-Semitic attacks throughout the city, organized firearms training classes, and took on the likes of neo-Nazi and other white-supremacist organizations, especially Holocaust deniers.

Irv was originally from Montreal and witnessed horrifying anti-Semitism as he was growing up. His Jewish identity grew stronger throughout the years. Having met Holocaust survivors and having heard their testimonies of the atrocities that they personally experienced and witnessed, Irv always had the brutal memories of the Holocaust etched in his mind and heart. He was determined to never allow his People to be victimized by haters again.

RB: How should the world remember Irv Rubin? What should we all know about him?

FS: I think that is best summed up in an article that I wrote about Irv after his death.

————

"Goodbye to a Jewish Hero"
The Jewish Press
By Fern Sidman
December 20, 2002

Irv Rubin was above all my good and close friend for better than 20 years. I first met him in the late-1970s when he visited New York City on JDL business. I'll always remember his warmth, his passion, and zeal for his People, his complete and utter devotion to JDL, and his sincere and heartfelt sensitivity to Jewish suffering.

I knew a man who did not possess any fear of his enemies. And believe me, those enemies were quite numerous and very vocal: Nazis and skinheads, Holocaust revisionists and Klansmen, Arab terrorists and Soviet operatives – even, sad to say, some elements of the Jewish establishment.

Irv never cowered in fear, he never retreated from his righteous position. He stood firm and stared his enemies in the face. That was Irv Rubin. A man who never batted an eyelash about getting in the middle of a confrontation with all sorts of white supremacists; a man who never showed any ambivalence about bringing issues before a court of law and using the legal system to fight his battles; a man who was indeed a lonely voice in the wilderness.

Irv was the very embodiment of the concept of *Ahavat Yisrael* – love of the Jewish people, love of the land of Israel, love of the G-d of Israel. Irv was a proud Zionist, never more so than when Vanessa Redgrave publicly called him a "Zionist hoodlum." Irv was a proud Jew, even when Nazi thugs threatened to turn him into a lampshade. That was Irv Rubin.

Most of all, I'll always remember the places Irv and I demonstrated together for Jewish causes.

Jewish history will, please G-d, record all his noble deeds. If our children ask us to describe the concept of *Ahavat Yisrael*, if they ask us to describe the true meaning of Jewish activism, if they ask us about the heroes of our people, we need only point to the living legacy of Irv Rubin. A man who exemplified bravery, courage, devotion, and unbounded love of his people, his family, his friends. A beloved husband and father, a tireless Jewish fighter. That was Irv Rubin.

Goodbye, my friend Irv. You are sorely, sorely missed. Until we meet again.

——

RB: How did your involvement in Betar and The Jewish Defense League shape you as the person and the Jew that you are today?

FS: I guess the answer would be: How didn't Betar and JDL help to define the person that I am? In Betar, I finally found my identity as a Jew, a Zionist, and a member of a proud organization that was formed to defend our People and sacrifice for the one and only Jewish state. It was in a Betar that I learned the personal power of belonging to a family of brothers and sisters that comprised the Jewish nation. I learned of the concept of *Hadar*, of the great pride of being a Jew, and behaving with self-respect, with courtesy, and decency while constantly taking the moral

high ground. I learned of the concept of Tagar, of
knowing that our role as Jews is to put body and mind on
the front lines, to never cower in fear, to know that
remaining silent in the face of adversity is unacceptable.

In JDL, I learned of the greatness of G-d
and Torah and that the ultimate objective of our
lives is not to constantly quench our own
hedonistic desires [but to] discipline ourselves to
become part of a cause far larger than ourselves. I
learned that each Jew has a part to play in the
tapestry of history; we each have our strengths and
weaknesses and we must use our strengths to help
our People while working on empowering
ourselves by overcoming our weaknesses. I learned
that this life that *HaShem* gave me does not belong
to me alone but rather to serving G-d in every way
by adhering to His laws, His dictums and decrees,
and His *mitzvos*. I learned that a Jew is endowed
with mercy and compassion and that we must use
this trait to comfort, strengthen, and heal our
People. I learned that a Jew behaves like a *mensch* (a
righteous person) at all times and that we are all
soldiers in G-d's army.

RB: Thank you, Fern, for your time and for being such an
inspiration to this project.

EPILOGUE: RABBI MEIR KAHANE

"What can we do today in Rabbi Kahane's absence? What can one say about the kind of man who will surely not arise again in our lifetime, until the messiah arrives?"

Donny Fuchs, Jewish Columnist

On the evening of November 5, 1990, Rabbi Meir Kahane gave a speech at a prominent hotel in Manhattan, New York. With wit, with anger, and with great humanity,

The great Rabbi Kahane

Rabbi Kahane challenged his audience to examine the perils of assimilation, the very real dangers of remaining silent in the face of evil, and how the new strong Jew of The JDL was really the old heroic Jew of the Torah reborn.

At the conclusion of his remarks, the Rabbi was met with thunderous applause; soon, a crowd of well-wishers gathered around Rabbi Kahane, congratulating him and asking additional questions. Blending into this group of supporters was a Muslim man of Egyptian descent dressed as an Orthodox Jew. Pretending to have a question for the Rabbi, the man stepped forward and shot Meir Kahane in the neck. The hall erupted into pandemonium and members of The Jewish Defense League scrambled to chase down and catch the assassin.

The great Rabbi, although struck in the throat, still managed to say, "*Shema Yisrael*," as he lay dying on his back.

The last word Rabbi Meir Kahane ever spoke was "Israel."

Israel.

The Land God chose for his Chosen People.

The Promised Land promising freedom, strength, majority, and self-determination.

The dream of, at long last, a home.

"*Shema Yisrael*
Adonai Elohaynu
Adonai Echad
Hear, O Israel
The Lord our God
The Lord is one."

The Shema prayer appears in Deuteronomy as an affirmation of the Jewish covenant with God and as a declaration of faith that there is but one God above.

It is Jewish tradition to say the *Shema* prayer before death.

During the Bar Kokhba revolt in 132 C.E., **Rabbi Akiva** recited the *Shema* while being tortured and executed by the Romans.

In the Nazi concentration camps, Jews recited the *Shema* in the gas chambers, while standing before firing squads, and as nooses were placed around their necks for hanging.

The *Shema* was the centerpiece of the last speech Moses gave to the Israelites before they went down into the Promised Land. Knowing he would not live to make the final journey with them, Moses blessed his People and trusted that they would thrive in his absence as free men and women responsible for their own lives in their own Land.

On the subject of his own death, Rabbi Kahane once remarked, "Someday I will have to face a Judge, and

with Him there will be, I believe, a great many souls. And I believe those souls stand by His side and when every Jew comes, they have a question that they pose to the soul that has just arrived. And that question is: 'Where were you when we cried out?' I want to be able to say I was there and I did what I could."

Like Moses' last words at Mount Nebo, Rabbi Kahane's final blessing to his followers was similarly a reminder of the dreams that remain for us to actualize in his absence.

The dreams that Rabbi Kahane dreamed require action.

Can his mission live on? The righteous live on as long as we give their teachings life.

The work continues.

It's not too late.

CONCLUSION

This book has taken you from the past to the present; and now, dear reader, the future is in your hands. Please consider devoting your energies from this day forward to honoring the great Rabbi Kahane who gave his very life for the dignity and survival of the Jewish People. Let his Warrior spirit ignite the brave Warrior inside of you. In his honor, stand tall and be proud: Jewish Is Beautiful.

Please consider committing yourself to living a full and proud Jewish life for the six million Jews whose lives were tragically cut short in the Holocaust.

Please consider donating a portion of your Bar or Bat Mitzvah gift money to an agency that supports the safety of Israel, such as "Friends of the IDF."

Please commit to participating in a Birthright Israel trip following graduation from high school so you can experience the Land that God promised your People firsthand.

Make a commitment to defending Israel against the lies that will undoubtedly be spouted on your college campus, including those from anti-Israel Jewish groups.

Make a commitment, when in the voting booth, to only ever support politicians (Jewish or non-Jewish) who stand with Israel. Always remember the Jewish Warrior decision-making yardstick: "Is it good for the Jews?" Forget about being loyal to a political party; be loyal to your People.

Make a commitment to raise your children in the Jewish faith.

Make a commitment to teach your children the truth about Israel.

Make a commitment to educate your children about their place in the lineage of Jewish Warriors since the time of Abraham.

Make a commitment to consciously connect your future to the past.

May God bless you and may you stand forever tall.

Rabbi Kahane and members of The JDL: "L'Chaim!"

SUGGESTED READING

The Story of The Jewish Defense League
Rabbi Meir Kahane
Chilton Book Company, 1975

Never Again!
Rabbi Meir Kahane
Nash Publishing, 1971

Rabbi Meir Kahane: His Life and Thought Volume One: 1932 – 1975
Libby Kahane
Institute for the Publication of the Writings of Rabbi Meir Kahane, 2008

Rabbi Meir Kahane: His Life and Thought Volume Two: 1976-1983
Libby Kahane
Institute for the Publication of the Writings of Rabbi Meir Kahane, 2015

Beyond Words: Rabbi Meir Kahane - Selected Writings Series
Rabbi Meir Kahane
Institute for the Publication of the Writings of Rabbi Meir Kahane, 2010

Listen World, Listen Jew
Rabbi Meir Kahane
Desert Ulpan of the Institute of the Jewish Idea, 1978

The Israel Warrior

Rabbi Shmuley Boteach
Gefen Publishing, 2016

Winning A Debate with An Israel-Hater
Dr. Michael Harris
Shorehouse Books, 2015

The Case For Israel
Alan Dershowitz
Wiley Books, 2003

Myths and Facts: A Guide to the Arab-Israeli Conflict
Mitchell G. Bard
AICE Books, 2006

The Jewish Book of Why
Alfred J. Kolatch
Jonathan David Publishers, 1982

Israel, A Nation of Warriors
Moshe Katz
Israeli Krav Maga International, 2015

Warfare in the Old Testament
Boyd Seevers
Kregel Publications, 2013

*Up, Up and Oy Vey: How Jewish History, Culture and Values
Shaped the Comic Book Superhero*
Rabbi Simcha Weinstein
Leviathon Press, 2006

Why the Jews? The Reason for Antisemitism
Dennis Prager and Joseph Telushkin
Touchstone Books, 2003

Night
Elie Wiesel
Bantam Books, 1960

Maus
Art Speigelman
Pantheon Books, 1973

The Book Thief
Markus Zusak
Picador Books, 2005

Nightfather
Carl Friedman
Parsea Books, 1991

SUGGESTED VIEWING

Schindler's List
Directed by Steven Spielberg
Universal Pictures, 1994

The Diary of Anne Frank
Directed by George Stevens
20th Century Fox, 1959

Paper Clips
Directed by Elliot Berlin and Joe Fab
Ergo Entertainment, 2004

Escape from Sobibor
Directed by Jack Gold
Zenith Entertainment, 1987

Defiance
Directed by Edward Zwick
Paramount Vantage, 2008

Skokie
Directed by Herbert Wise
Titus Productions, 1981

The Chosen
Directed by Jeremy Kagan
20th Century Fox, 1982

Fiddler on the Roof
Directed by Norman Jewison

United Artists, 1971

Exodus
Directed by Otto Preminger
United Artists, 1960

The Ten Commandments
Directed by Cecil B. DeMille
Paramount Pictures, 1956

BIBLIOGRAPHY

Interior Quote

Kahane, Rabbi Meir. Never Again! A Program for Survival pg.
     244. Los Angeles: Nash Publishing, 1971.

Introduction

Bernstein, Fred. *The Jewish Mothers' Hall of Fame.* Garden City, NY:
     Doubleday & Company, Inc., 1986. P. 139.
Candace Owens, Twitter post, September 22, 2018, 1238.
     https://twitter.com/realcandaceo/status/1043555129322
     921985?lang=en.
Gill, Julian. "The KISS Album Focus." *San Francisco:
     KISSFAQ.com*, 2002. P. 99.
Kahane, Libby. *Rabbi Meir Kahane: His Life and Thoughts, Volume
     One: 1932-1975.* Jerusalem, Israel: Institute for Publication
     of the Writings of Rabbi Meir Kahane, 2008. P. 7.
Kahane, Rabbi Meir. *The Story of The Jewish Defense League.* Radnor,
     PN: Chilton Book Company, 1978. P. 73, 74, 77, 86, 141,
     205, 207, 221, 226, 263, 304.
TV View. "Trivializing the Holocaust: Semi-Fact and Semi-
     Fiction." *The New York Times* (New York, NY), April 16,
     1978. P. 75.

Preface: Key Principles of the Jewish Warrior

Kahane, Rabbi Meir. *Never Again! A Program for Survival.* Los
     Angeles, CA: Nash Publishing, 1971. P. 118.
Kahane, Rabbi Meir. *The Story of The Jewish Defense League.* Radnor,
     PN: Chilton Book Company, 1978. P. 90.

Mars, Rabbi Sharon. "Israel." *Temple Israel.* Yom Kippur Morning
    Sermon, 2018. Accessed: September 29, 2020.
    https://www.templeisrael.org/rabbis-message.
Torossian, Ronn. "Menachem Begin to Joe Biden: I Am Not a
    Jew with Trembling Knees." *JewishPress.com.* April 3, 2015.
    http://www.jewishpress.com/indepth/opinions/menache
    m-begin-to-joe-biden-i-am-not-a-jew-with-trembling-
    knees/2015/04/03.

Real-Life Superheroes: Warriors of the Bible

Boteach, Rabbi Shmuley. *The Israel Warrior: Fighting Back for the
    Jewish State from Campus to Street Corner.* Jerusalem, Israel:
    Gefen Publishing House Limited, 2016. P. 3.
Kahane, Rabbi Meir. *Listen World, Listen Jew.* Tucson, AZ: Desert
    Ulpan of the Institute of the Jewish Idea, 1978. P. 29.
The Phil Donahue Show. Broadcasted on January 21, 1981.
    "Irving Rubin – Jewish Tradition Isn't About Giving the
    Other Cheek, But About Fighting Back." *BitChute.com,*
    9:07. December 10, 2019.
    https://www.bitchute.com/video/V3ab3aGUdLBG/
Rock, Lois. Christina Balit. *The Lion Illustrated Bible for Children.*
    London, UK: Mayfield House, 2005. P. 90.
Samuels, Ruth. *Bible Stories for Jewish Children.* New York, NY: Ktav
    Publishing House, 1954.
Seevers, Boyd. *Warfare in the Old Testament: The Organization,
    Weapons, and Tactics of Ancient Near Eastern Armies.* Grand
    Rapids, CO: Kregel Publications, 2013. P. 62-65.
Weilerstein, Sadie Rose. *Jewish Heroes: Book One.* New York, NY:
    United Synagogue Commission on Jewish Education,
    1953. P. 121-122, 136, 140-141, 148-149, 154.
Weinstein, Rabbi Simcha. *Up, Up, and Oy Vey: How Jewish History,
    Cultures, and Values Shaped the Comic Book Superhero.* Fort
    Lee, NJ: Barricade Books, 2006. P. 21.

Moses

Fisher, Leonard Everett. *Moses*. New York, NY: Holiday House,
        1995. P. 4.
Samuels, Ruth. *Bible Stories for Jewish Children*. New York, NY: Ktav
        Publishing House, 1954. P. 49, 51, 64.
Weilerstein, Sadie Rose. *Jewish Heroes: Book One*. New York, NY:
        United Synagogue Commission on Jewish Education,
        1953. P. 95, 110.

Kahane Korner: Aiding and Defending Fellow Jews

Kahane, Rabbi Meir. *Never Again! A Program for Survival*. Los
        Angeles, CA: Nash Publishing, 1971. P. 147-148.
Kahane, Rabbi Meir. *The Story of The Jewish Defense League*. Radnor,
        PN: Chilton Book Company, 1978. P. 80, 142.

David

Chamberlin, Anne. "Israel Onrush." *Vogue*. July 1969. P. 106-107.
Rock, Lois. Christina Balit. *The Lion Illustrated Bible for Children*.
        London, UK: Mayfield House, 2005. P. 104.
Samuels, Ruth. *Bible Stories for Jewish Children*. New York, NY: Ktav
        Publishing House, 1954.
Schenk de Reigniers, Beatrice. *David and Goliath*. New York, NY:
        Orchard Books, 1993. P. 7, 9, 22-24.
Weilerstein, Sadie Rose. *Jewish Heroes: Book One*. New York, NY:
        United Synagogue Commission on Jewish Education,
        1953. P. 175, 191.

Kahane Korner: Jews and Weapons

"Nothing Says 'Never Again Like an Armed Jew.'" Jews Can
        Shoot. Accessed: September 29, 2020.
        https://jewscanshoot.com.

Halkin, Hillel. *Jabotinsky: A Life*. New Haven, CT and London, UK: Yale University Press, 2014. P. 121.

Kahane, Libby. *Rabbi Meir Kahane: His Life and Thoughts, Volume One: 1932-1975*. Jerusalem, Israel: Institute for Publication of the Writings of Rabbi Meir Kahane, 2008. P. 96, 114.

The Phil Donahue Show. Broadcasted on January 21, 1981. "Irving Rubin – Jewish Tradition Isn't About Giving the Other Cheek, But About Fighting Back." *BitChute.com*, 9:07. December 10, 2019.

Esther

Rock, Lois. Christina Balit. *The Lion Illustrated Bible for Children*. London, UK: Mayfield House, 2005. P. 104, 149.

Weilerstein, Sadie Rose. *Jewish Heroes: Book One*. New York, NY: United Synagogue Commission on Jewish Education, 1953. P. 131-132.

Weilerstein, Sadie Rose. *Jewish Heroes: Book Two*. New York, NY: United Synagogue Commission on Jewish Education, 1956. P. 134, 135-140, 145.

Kahane Korner: Jewish Identity and Pride

Halevi, Yossi Klein. *Memoirs of a Jewish Extremist*. Boston, MA: Little, Brown, and Company, 1995. P. 107, 119, 142.

Kahane, Libby. *Rabbi Meir Kahane: His Life and Thoughts, Volume One: 1932-1975*. Jerusalem, Israel: Institute for Publication of the Writings of Rabbi Meir Kahane, 2008. P. 63.

Kolatch, Alfred J. *The Jewish Book of Why*. New York, NY: Jonathan David Publishers, Inc., 1981. P. 121-122.

Judah Maccabee

Halevi, Yossi Klein. *Memoirs of a Jewish Extremist*. Boston, MA: Little, Brown, and Company, 1995. P. 79.

Stoddard, Sandol. *A Child's First Bible Storybook*. New York, NY: Inspirational Press, 1990. P. 59.

Weilerstein, Sadie Rose. *Jewish Heroes: Book Two*. New York, NY: United Synagogue Commission on Jewish Education, 1956. P. 146, 149, 151, 154, 155.

Kahane Korner: Jews and the Use of Physical Strength

Aleph Society, Inc. Accessed October 12, 2020. https://steinsaltz.org/.

Daniels, Jeff, dir. *Mother with a Gun*. Australia: Common Rooms Productions in association with Unicorn Films, 2016. Netflix.

Dolgin, Janet L. *Jewish Identity and The JDL*. Princeton, NJ: Princeton University Press, 1977. P. 23.

Stoddard, Sandol. *A Child's First Bible Storybook*. New York, NY: Inspirational Press, 1990. P. 59.

Masada

Bar-am, Aviva and Shmuel. "Masada, Tragic Fortress in the Sky." *The Times of Israel.* April 13, 2013. https://www.timesofisrael.com/masada-tragic-fortress-in-the-sky/

Gottlieb, Gerald. *The Story of Masada*. New York, NY: Random House, 1969. P. 75, 78, 114, 130.

Iglitzen-Socianu, Cindy. "Masada: A Symbol of Jewish Freedom." *Israel Advantage Tours.* May 30. Year Unknown. Accessed: October 5, 2020. https://www.israeladvantagetours.com/masada-symbol-jewish-freedom/.

Kahane, Libby. *Rabbi Meir Kahane: His Life and Thoughts, Volume One: 1932-1975.* Jerusalem, Israel: Institute for Publication of the Writings of Rabbi Meir Kahane, 2008. P. 236.

Samuels, Ruth. *Bible Stories for Jewish Children*. New York, NY: Ktav
    Publishing House, 1954. P. 49.
Weilerstein, Sadie Rose. *Jewish Heroes: Book Two*. New York, NY:
    United Synagogue Commission on Jewish Education,
    1956. P. 148.

Kahane Korner: Refusing to Die on Our Enemies' Terms

Rock, Lois. Christina Balit. *The Lion Illustrated Bible for Children*.
    London, UK: Mayfield House, 2005. P. 92.
Weilerstein, Sadie Rose. *Jewish Heroes: Book Two*. New York, NY:
    United Synagogue Commission on Jewish Education,
    1956. P. 149, 154.

Real-life Superheroes: Warriors Leading Up To and During the Holocaust

Ades, Lisa, dir. *GI Jews: Jewish Americans in World War II*. New
    York, NY: Thirteen Productions in association with
    Turquoise Films, 2018.
Bukiet, Melvin Jules. *Nothing Makes You Free: Writing by Descendants
    of Jewish Holocaust Survivors*. New York, NY: W.W. Norton
    & Company, Inc., 2002.
Chards, María Isabel Carrasco Cara. "Meet the Ballerina Who
    Shot a Nazi and Started a Riot in Auschwitz." *Cultura
    Colectiva*. December 17, 2017.
    http://culturacolectiva.com/history/franceska-mann-
    auschwitz-riot-ballerina.
Friedman, Carl. *Nightfather*. New York, NY: Persea Books, 1995.
Klee, Ernst, and Willi Dressen, and Volkier Reiss. *The Good Old
    Days: The Holocaust as Seen by Its Perpetrators and Bystanders*.
    New York: NY: Konecky and Konecky, 1991. P. XX.
Posner, Gerald L., and John Ware. *Mengele: The Complete Story*. New
    York, NY: McGraw-Hill Book Company, 1986. P. 324.

Prager, Dennis. "You Can Kill, But Not Murder: The Case for the Ten Commandments." Prager's Column. *The Dennis Prager Show*. December 2, 2014. https://dennisprager.com/column/can-kill-not-murder-case-ten-commandments/.

Ze'ev Jabotinsky

Halkin, Hillel. *Jabotinsky: A Life*. New Haven, CT and London, England: Yale University Press, 2014. P. 57, 207, 121, 171.
Jewish Virtual Library. "Ze'ev (Vladimir) Jabotinsky: 1880-1940." Accessed: October 5, 2020. https://www.jewishvirtuallibrary.org/ze-ev-vladimir-jabotinsky.
Kahane, Libby. *Rabbi Meir Kahane: His Life and Thoughts, Volume One: 1932-1975*. Jerusalem, Israel: Institute for Publication of the Writings of Rabbi Meir Kahane, 2008. P. 5, 7, 288.
Schwartz, E.A. Private audio interview with Rabbi Meir Kahane in New York, January 1975. Unpublished. Sent to author as a CD on February 2, 2015.

Kahane Korner: Rabbi Kahane on Ze'ev Jabotinsky

Halevi, Yossi Klein, and Yôsî Qlayn hal- Lēwî. *Memoirs of a Jewish Extremist*. Boston, MA: Little, Brown and Company, 1995. P. 36.

Sobibor Concentration Camp

NewsMaxWorld. "On Holocaust Day, Netanyahu Says Its Lessons Guide Him." April 23, 2017. https://www.newsmax.com/World/MiddleEast/ML-Israel-Holocaust/2017/04/23/id/785893/.
Wiesel, Elie. *Night*. New York, NY: Bantam Books, 1960. P. 36, 39.

Rashke, Richard. *Escape from Sobibor.* Urbana and Chicago:
        University of Illinois Press, 1982. P. 202, 203, 213, 215,
        229, 231, 271.
Bukiet, Melvin Jules. *Nothing Makes You Free: Writing by Descendants
        of Jewish Holocaust Survivors.* New York, NY: W.W. Norton
        & Company, Inc., 2002.
Spiegelman, Art. *Maus.* New York, NY: Pantheon Books, 1986.
Gold, Jack, dir. *Escape from Sobibor.* La Crosse, WI: Echo Bridge,
        1987. Film.

Jewish Resistance Fighters

Boteach, Rabbi Shmuley. "On Israel's Independence Day: The
        Little Country That Could." *Observer.com.* May 13, 2016.
        https://observer.com/2016/05/on-israels-independence-
        day-the-little-country-that-could/.
Jewish Partisan Educational Foundation. "What Is a Jewish
        Partisan?" Accessed: October 5, 2020.
        http://www.jewishpartisans.org/what-is-a-jewish-partisan
Kahane, Rabbi Meir. *The Story of The Jewish Defense League.* Radnor,
        PN: Chilton Book Company, 1975. P. 129.

Kahane Korner: The Jewish Warrior and Self-Control

Jewish Partisan Educational Foundation. "What Is a Jewish
        Partisan?" Accessed: October 5, 2020.
        http://www.jewishpartisans.org/what-is-a-jewish-partisan
Kahane, Rabbi Meir. *Listen World, Listen Jew.* Jerusalem, Israel:
        Institute for Publication of the Writings of Rabbi Meir
        Kahane, 2011. P. 217- 219.
"Interview: Meir Kahane, a Candid Conversation with the Militant
        Leader of the Jewish Defense League." *Playboy.* October
        1972. P. 75.

Kahane, Meir. *Beyond Words: Selected Writings 1960-1973 (Volume 1).* Jerusalem, Israel: Institute for Publication of the Writings of Rabbi Meir Kahane, 2010.

Warsaw Ghetto Uprising

Hersey, John. *The Wall.* New York, NY: Knopf Book Club, 1980.
"The Warsaw Resistance…" Irv Rubin on The Phil Donahue Show. US: January 21, 1981.
Landau, Elaine. *The Warsaw Ghetto Uprising.* New York, NY: Macmillan Publishing Company, 1992. P. 5, 6, 7, 14, 50, 69.
United States Holocaust Memorial Musueum, Washington, D.C. "Warsaw Ghetto Uprising." Accessed: October 5, 2020. https://encyclopedia.ushmm.org/content/en/article/warsaw-ghetto-uprising.

Real-life Superheroes: In the Aftermath of the Holocaust

Dolgin, Janet L. *Jewish Identity and The JDL.* Princeton, NJ: Princeton University Press, 1977. P. 87.

Nazi Hunters

United States Holocaust Museum, Washington, D.C. "Nazi Hunting: Simon Wiesenthal." Accessed: October 5, 2020. https://encyclopedia.ushmm.org/content/en/article/nazi-hunting-simon-wiesenthal.
Freedland, Johnathan. "Revenge." *The Guardian.* July 25, 2018. https://www.theguardian.com/world/2008/jul/26/second.world.war.
Wiesenthal, Simon. *The Murderers Among Us: The Simon Wiesenthal Memoirs.* New York, NY: McGraw-Hill, 1967.
Nagorski, Andrew. *The Nazi Hunters.* New York, NY: Simon & Schuster, 2017.

Kahane Korner: Vigilantism

Kahane, Rabbi Meir. *Never Again! A Program for Survival.* Los
    Angeles, CA: Nash Publishing, 1971. P. 160.
Kahane, Rabbi Meir. *The Story of The Jewish Defense League.* Radnor,
    PN: Chilton Book Company, 1975. P. 220-221.

Menachem Begin

Bard, Mitchell G. *Myths and Facts: A Guide to the Arab-Israeli Conflict.*
    Chevy Chase, MD: American Israeli Cooperative
    Enterprise (AICE), 2006, 2017. P. 1.
Brackett, Virginia, *Menachem Begin.* Philadelphia, PN: Chelsea
    House Books, 2003. P. 20, 31, 34, 100.
History of Israel. "The History of Israel – A Chronological
    Presentation." Accessed: October 5, 2020. http://history-
    of-israel.org/history/chronological_presentation21.php.
Kahane, Rabbi Meir. *The Story of The Jewish Defense League.* Radnor,
    PN: Chilton Book Company, 1975. P. 55.
Wolf, Joseph. "The Story of the Ship Exodus 1947." *World Machal.*
    Accessed: October 5, 2020.
    http://www.machal.org.il/index.php?option=com_conten
    t&view=article&id=557.

Zionism: Interview with Lauren Isaacs – Herut, Canada

Cohen, Karma Feinstein. 2020. "Herut North America
    #ZionUnite." *Facebook.* January 11, 2020.
    https://www.facebook.com/zionuniteherut/
Isaacs, Lauren. Private interview with author. Email. March 6,
    2020.

Kahane Korner: Jews and the Importance of Israel

Amler, Justin. "Why Anti-Zionists Are Absolutely Anti-Semites."
    Israellycool.com. October 2, 2018.
    https://www.israellycool.com/2018/10/02/why-anti-
    zionists-are-absolutely-antisemites/.
Kahane, Meir. *Beyond Words: Selected Writings 1960-1973 (Volume 1)*.
    Jerusalem, Israel: Institute for Publication of the Writings
    of Rabbi Meir Kahane, 2010.
Kahane, Rabbi Meir. *Listen World, Listen Jew*. Jerusalem, Israel:
    Institute for Publication of the Writings of Rabbi Meir
    Kahane, 2011. P. 29, 168, 228.
Kahane, Rabbi Meir. *The Story of The Jewish Defense League*. Radnor,
    PN: Chilton Book Company, 1975. P. 228.

Meir Kahane and The Jewish Defense League

Fern Sidman, interview by author. Email. June 26, 2019.

Kahane Korner: Martial Arts and the Jewish Warrior

Halevi, Yossi Klein, and Yôsî Qlayn hal- Lēwî. *Memoirs of a Jewish
    Extremist*. Boston, MA: Little, Brown and Company, 1995.
    P. 41.
Kahane, Libby. *Rabbi Meir Kahane: His Life and Thought, Volume
    One: 1932-1975*. Jerusalem, Israel: Institute for Publication
    of the Writings of Rabbi Meir Kahane, 2008. P. 114.
Katz, Moshe, interview by author. *Facebook*. Private Message. April
    15, 2019.
Krav Maga Mahopac. "What is Krav Maga?" Accessed: October
    6, 2020.
    https://kravmagamahopac.com/blog/73915/What-Is-
    Krav-Maga.
The Phil Donahue Show. Broadcasted on January 21, 1981.
    "Irving Rubin – Jewish Tradition Isn't About Giving the

Other Cheek, But About Fighting Back." *BitChute.com*,
9:07. December 10, 2019.

Irv Rubin

Sidman, Fern. "Goodbye to a Jewish Hero." *JewishPress.com*.
December 20, 2002.
https://www.jewishpress.com/indepth/opinions/goodby
e-to-a-jewish-hero/2002/12/20/.

Interview with Shelley Rubin

Shelley Rubin, interview by author. Las Vegas, NV, February 7,
2015.

Skokie

Alpert, Buzz. "Comparing Skokie to Charlottesville." *American
Thinker*. August 24, 2017.
https://www.americanthinker.com/articles/2017/08/com
paring_skokie_to_charlottesville_comments.html.
W Bez. "Street Fights with Chicago Neo-Nazis in the 1970s."
YouTube Video, 1:40, April 21, 2017.
https://www.youtube.com/watch?v=fzOWJTpbh94
Whitman, Todd, and Rick Hirschhaut. *Skokie: Invaded But Not
Conquered*. Illinois Holocaust Museum & Education
Center, 2014. DVD.

Kahane Korner: The Perils of Silence and Respectability

Kahane, Rabbi Meir. *Beyond Words: Selected Writings 1960-1973
(Volume 1)*. Jerusalem, Israel: Institute for Publication of
the Writings of Rabbi Meir Kahane, 2010.
Kahane, Rabbi Meir. *The Story of The Jewish Defense League*. Radnor,
PN: Chilton Book Company, 1975. P. 5, 42, 73, 117.

Israel Defense Forces

Bergman, Ronen. "The Secret History of Mossad, Israel's Feared and Respected Intelligence Agency." *Newstatesman.com.* August 15, 2018. https://www.newstatesman.com/world/middle-east/2018/08/secret-history-mossad-israel-s-feared-and-respected-intelligence-agency.

Blech, Rabbi Benjamin. "The Miracle of the Six-Day War." *GodReports.com.* June 8, 2017. http://godreports.com/2017/06/the-miracle-of-the-six-day-war/.

David Collier, Twitter Post, September 21, 2018. 0303. https://twitter.com/mishtal/status/1043078334270332928.

History.com Editors. "Six-Day War." *History.com.* August 21, 2018. https://www.history.com/topics/middle-east/six-day-war.

Encyclopedia Britannica. "Israel Defense Forces." Accessed: October 6, 2020. http://britannica.com/topic/Israel-Defense-Forces#info-article-history.

Israel Defense Force. "Eight Miraculous Moments in IDF History." December 17, 2014. https://www.idf.il/en/minisites/our-soldiers/8-miraculous-moments-in-idf-history/.

Jewish Virtual Library. "Israel Defense Forces: History & Overview." Accessed: October 6, 2020. https://www.jewishvirtuallibrary.org/history-and-overview-of-the-israel-defense-forces.

Kahane Korner: Passing the Torch

Kahane, Rabbi Meir. *Beyond Words: Selected Writings 1960-1973 (Volume 1).* Jerusalem, Israel: Institute for Publication of the Writings of Rabbi Meir Kahane, 2010. P. 208.

Modern-Day Jewish Defense League: International

Weinstein, Meir Halevi, interview by the author. *Facebook*. Private
     Message. August 1, 2019.
Hadida, Aharon, interview by the author. Facebook. Private
     Message. September 19, 2018.
Messchendorp, Tom, interview by the author. Facebook. Private
     Message. August 1, 2019.

Kahane Korner: A "Supermensch" for the Next Generation

Anderman, Nirit. "Supermensches: Comic Books' Secret Jewish
     History." *Haaretz*. January 24, 2016.
     https://www.haaretz.com/israel-
     news/culture/MAGAZINE-supermensches-comic-
     books-jewish-history-1.5393475.
Weinstein, Rabbi Simcha. *Up, Up, and Oy Vey: How Jewish History,
     Cultures, and Values Shaped the Comic Book Superhero.* Fort
     Lee, NJ: Barricade Books, 2006. P. 21.
Kaplan, Arie. *From Krakow to Krypton: Jews and Comic Books.*
     Philadelphia, PA: The Jewish Publication Society, 2008.

Zionist Biker Clubs

Goldberger, Nir, interview by the author. *Facebook*. Private
     Message. August 6, 2019.
Pearl, Judea. "Faculty Corner: Zionophobia – Our Only Fighting
     Word." *Ha'Am*. May 14, 20018.
     https://haam.org/zionophobia-our-only-fighting-word/.

Fern Sidman

Daniels, Jeff, dir. *Mother with a Gun*. Australia: Common Rooms
     Productions in association with Unicorn Films, 2016.
     Netflix.
Sidman, Fern. "Goodbye to a Jewish Hero." *JewishPress.com*.
     December 20, 2002.
     https://www.jewishpress.com/indepth/opinions/goodby
     e-to-a-jewish-hero/2002/12/20/.
Sidman, Fern, interview by the author. Email. June 26, 2019.

Epilogue: Rabbi Meir Kahane

Diamant, Anita. "Viddui: The Deathbed Confession."
     MyJewishLearning. Accessed: October 6, 2020.
     https://www.myjewishlearning.com/article/viddui-the-
     deathbed-confession/.
Fuchs, Donny. "Rabbi Meir Kahane: My Rebbe (That I
     Never Met)." *JewishPress.com*. November 10, 2014.
     https://www.jewishpress.com/indepth/columns/
     fuchs-focus/rabbi-meir-kahane-my-rebbe-that-i-
     never-met/2014/11/10/.
Kahane, Rabbi Meir. *Beyond Words: Selected Writings 1960-1973
     (Volume 1)*. Jerusalem, Israel: Institute for Publication of
     the Writings of Rabbi Meir Kahane, 2010. P. 215.
Kelman-Ezrachi, Rabbi Naamah. "Moses' Final Blessing." *My
     JewishLearning*. Accessed: October 6, 2020.
     https://www.myjewishlearning.com/article/the-final-
     blessing/.
Kifner, John. "Meir Kahane, 58, Israeli Militant and
     Founder of The Jewish Defense League." *The New
     York Times*, Section B, Page 13. November 6, 1990.
Neiman, Na'ama. *Miracle Man*. Jerusalem, Israel: Yeshiva
     of the Jewish Idea, 2010. P. 41.

ABOUT THE AUTHOR

Ross Berg is an empathic educator holding a Bachelor's Degree in English Literature and a Master's Degree in Counseling. His first book *Gene Simmons: A Rock 'N Roll Journey in the Shadow of the Holocaust* focuses on children of Holocaust survivors.

After exploring the tragic side of Jewish victimhood, Berg was ready to investigate the flipside of that topic by shedding light on the strength and heroism of the Jewish People – from the time of the bible to the modern era. Seeking to empower young people, Berg was moved to provide real-life examples of fearless and tenacious Jewish men and women who chose to walk tall and to live in pride as inspiring examples to us all.

ABOUT THE PHOTOGRAPHER

E.A. Schwartz began his career as a Photo Editor for the Associated Press. In the mid-1970s, Schwartz took a multitude of photographs documenting the activities of Rabbi Meir Kahane and The Jewish Defense League; in addition, he also conducted a series of interviews with the great Rabbi.

E.A. Schwartz recently retired from a distinguished career as a college professor. His photographs, taped interviews, and personal memories have contributed immeasurably to this book project.

ABOUT THE ARTIST

Always a creative spirit, Ken Mills is a graphic artist by trade. His work has been featured in magazines, books, comics, and in many logo designs. He is currently creating and designing gift bags and greeting cards for all seasons. He has also been a writer, musician, and comedian.

A lifelong comic book fan, Ken was thrilled to be asked to celebrate and shine a light on the heroes of Jewish culture. Ken's primary creative outlet is podcasting, which he has enjoyed for the last 14 years. Ken has built a great following with shows that focus on popular music, pop culture, and society.

Among his shows are "PodKISSt," "Cheap Talk," "Zilch: a Monkees Podcast," and "POP with Ken Mills."